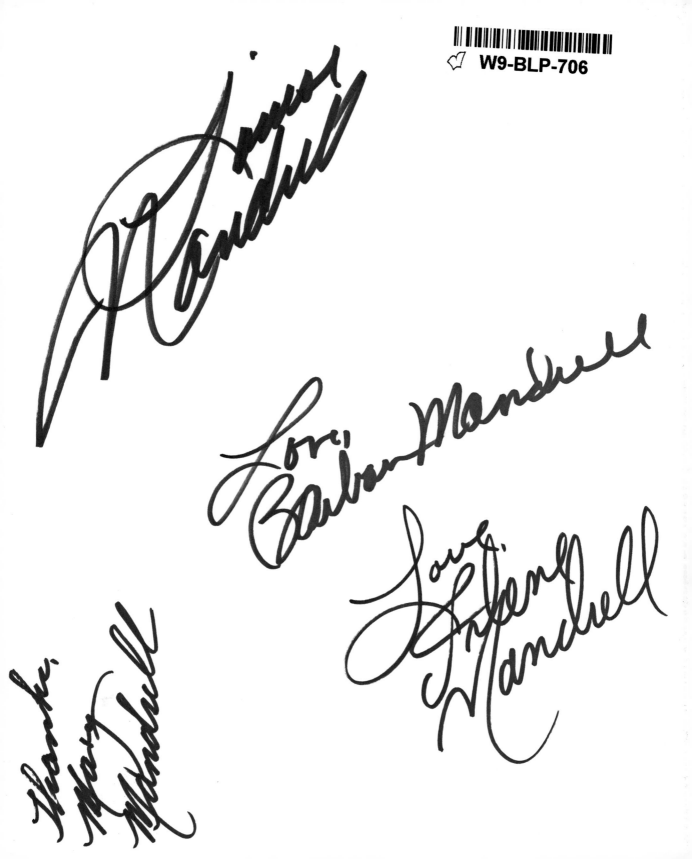

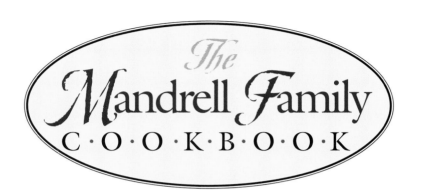

The
Mandrell Family
C·O·O·K·B·O·O·K

The Mandrell Family
C·O·O·K·B·O·O·K

MATTHEW DUDNEY

*With Barbara, Louise,
Irlene, and Mary Mandrell*

Foreword by
BARBARA MANDRELL

RUTLEDGE HILL PRESS®

Nashville, Tennessee

A Thomas Nelson Company

Published by Rutledge Hill Press®, a Thomas Nelson Company, P.O. Box 141000, Nashville, Tennessee 37214.

Cover photo by Rose Mason
Cover and text design by Gore Design Studio
Typography by Roger A. DeLiso, Rutledge Hill Press®
Family photographs by the authors unless otherwise noted
Food photographs by Rose Mason

Library of Congress Cataloging-in-Publication Data:
Dudney, Matt, 1970–
    The Mandrell family cookbook / Matt Dudney, with Barbara, Louise, Irlene, and Mary Mandrell.
      p.   cm.
   Includes index.
   ISBN 1-55853-752-X
   1. Cookery.   I. Title.
TX714.D84   1999
641.5—dc21   99-28592
                        CIP

Printed in the United States of America
3 4 5 6 7 8 9—08 07 06 05 04

To my parents, who have always been there for me. No one could ask for parents more dedicated to their children. May God bless you as He has blessed me with you.

Contents

Acknowledgments

I would like to start by thanking my Aunt Louise for coming up with the idea of writing a cookbook. It sure grew into something wonderful.

Thank you so much to my family for sharing your memories with me so that I might share them with those who read this book.

To Angie Gore, for introducing me to the patient and creative people at Rutledge Hill Press; you have always been so wonderful to my family.

To my Uncle Alan Siegel and Bob Stein; I cannot begin to thank you enough. I owe you both big time.

I would especially like to thank Uncle Larry and Clay for all of their hard work and perseverance; I know that it wasn't easy.

To Rose; you take the best photographs and I can't wait to work together again.

Jim, you are the best; keep that bullet shiny.

To Leigh Ann; thank you for making each day special. I love you.

Most of all, thank you to the Lord God for all good things.

Foreword

My children have been a source of constant amazement to me throughout my years. Here I am telling you about my phenomenal son Matthew, who over the years has given his family nothing but love and respect. If he's not working with us in Nashville, he's involved in the New York food scene—recently helping his friend, Chef Danny Egnezzo, cook for an important event honoring Tommy Hilfiger. Whatever happened to the little boy who yelled, "Ah! Ah!" as we walked through the grocery store, so that I would buy him some green "Ah-lives"? Or the teenager who told us he was going to fix fajitas for dinner, and did a marvelous job, not telling us until later that he had never made them before? Time sure goes by fast. I have tried to teach him the many things that he will need in life, but in the kitchen, he teaches me. This wonderful cookbook is not only laced with many personal memories and pictures, but it is also very useful in the way that the recipes are put together. The writing, compiling, and whatever else happens in a project such as this cookbook are mostly a mystery to me, but I believe that Matthew has done a marvelous job. Now I can throw away all those recipes which Matthew has written on little pieces of paper for me and use this beautiful book.

Matthew presenting his mother with a Mother's Day gift, 1983.

I take pride in using Matthew's cookbook in my kitchen, and I'm thrilled by the compliments I get. I know that you will be proud to have this book and share its recipes with your friends and families, too. Matthew has provided a way for all of us to have a good visit, over good food.

*I*ntroduction

*I*n *The Mandrell Family Cookbook* you will find recipes from my mother Barbara, her sisters Louise and Irlene, my grandmother Mary, and also some of my own creations. Many of the recipes reflect our southern heritage and influences, and many are intensely simple and practical, since we know what it's like to be busy and not have much time in the kitchen.

There are stories and photographs of what it's been like to grow up in a busy and famous musical family, which still emphasizes spending time together. The stories are personal and for the most part have not been told in magazines or interviews. They're about real life, including the years on the road, how we spend the holidays, and the things we do and the places we go to relax and unwind.

My grandfather Irby is from Arkansas and met my grandmother in a small church in Illinois. After they married, they moved to Texas where all the Mandrell girls were born. Many of these stories are about my mother, the oldest of the three sisters. She was born when my grandmother was only seventeen years old. Her sister Louise came along when Mom was almost six, and Irlene, the youngest, was born eighteen months later.

Mary and Irby made music an integral part of their lives from the very beginning. Mom began playing music at the age of ten and it wasn't long before my grandfather formed the Mandrell Family Band. My grandmother played bass guitar; my grandfather was the leader of the band, the singer, and the rhythm guitar player; Mom

Irby leading the Mandrell Family Band.

played the steel guitar, banjo, and saxophone. My dad Ken was hired as a drummer by my grandfather, and he and Mom were married about six months after she turned eighteen.

Dad was a Navy pilot, so Mom retired from show business. However, with the music still in her heart and soul, Mom couldn't completely divorce herself from entertaining. When Dad went overseas on an aircraft carrier, Mom organized a band called the Do-Rites. Louise played bass and Irlene played the drums. They toured where they could and worked in Europe for the military. From there they became "Barbara Mandrell and the Mandrell Sisters" and NBC aired them in the early 1980s as the last successful variety show.

Mom did her last touring concert in October 1997 and now devotes her time and energy toward acting in television and movies. My dad is a successful businessman.

I was born in 1970 and spent several years of my life on the family bus, traveling up and down the road with my mom. My sister Jaime took my place on the bus just in time for me to start school. Now she's an actor in New York on the popular soap opera *As the World Turns.* My brother Nathan, a teenager, is fast becoming a great ice hockey player and is already investigating what college to attend.

Louise devotes the majority of her time to a musical theater in Pigeon Forge, Tennessee, called "The Louise Mandrell Theater." During the off-season, she tours the country, performing and entertaining for those who can't be in Tennessee to see her. She is actively involved in raising money for the Boy Scouts with a celebrity shotgun shoot every year.

Irlene races Legend Cars and volunteers for several charities, along with making numerous personal appearances around the country.

My grandparents are now basically retired (oh sure), so it's still possible for all of

Matthew, the young gourmet.

us to get together, sit down, visit, and have a great meal once in a while.

I became interested in cooking, as most children seem to do, at an early age. Some of my greatest memories growing up were of the times we spent around the table, even when we were on the road. When I was about sixteen years old, cooking took on a whole new meaning for me as I realized that preparing a delicious meal was the best way to impress a girl. It seemed to work, most of the time. Later I discovered that a delicious meal could be the key to anyone's heart.

Creating food for people who are important to you makes the work meaningful and much more enjoyable. I know that anyone who cooks finds no greater pleasure than seeing family and friends enjoy a meal that was especially prepared for them.

If you don't enjoy cooking, then it's possible you're trying too hard. Cooking can and should be fun—and mostly easy. That's the point of this book. You'll learn shortcuts that make cooking simpler and recipes that give you reliable results. All the ingredients used in this book (except for wild game) are available in your local grocery store, which makes the shopping experience much less of a drudgery.

You'll also learn about our family and the joys we have discovered by preparing and enjoying meals together. Eating together has always been important to our family, so we truly hope that the stories and the recipes we have shared here will make cooking as enjoyable for you as it has been for all of us.

The most important ingredient in family cooking . . . is fun!

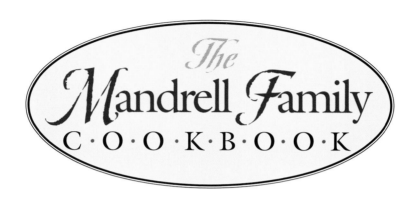

Barbara, the bride; Charline, the flower girl (Ken's half-sister);
and Louise and Irlene, the junior bridesmaids.

Newlyweds
Hard Times and Burnt Food

You might think this is chauvinistic, but the truth is many single women around my age, say 24 to 30, really don't know how to cook. However, I often (facetiously) defend my sister Jaime. "After all," I always point out, "Jaime *does* know how to boil water." In all fairness, most guys my age don't know how to cook either, but for some reason we expect women to know more.

Of course, it's not just single women and it's not just modern women (and men) who aren't born cooks. Times haven't changed *that* much. But everyone can *become* a good cook. All it takes is desire, practice, and a "guinea pig" who loves you and is willing to taste your creations.

With that said, I can admit that, when the women in my family first got married, they didn't really know how to cook. Many of the stories in this chapter are about the ruined meals that nevertheless are the roots to some delicious family recipes—and stories.

And there are plenty of happy endings. Today, Mom is an excellent cook. Louise particularly likes to express her love for children by making fun food. And Irlene, who is a conservationist and a hunter, enjoys trying new ways to cook venison or quail.

When the women in our family first got married, they didn't really know how to cook.

..ry, the Mandrell family matriarch, can still cook food the way most Southern men remember their grandmothers' cooking. She makes the best fried pork chops you'll ever have the pleasure of tasting. I asked my grandfather Irby whether she was a bad cook when they first got married. "She was actually a *wonderful* cook," he replied without hesitation. (Well, you say, there goes my whole premise that most Mandrell women start out not being able to cook. But my grandfather is a wily man of great wisdom who's had years of training and knows precisely what response will defuse any potentially explosive question.)

Even as a young newlywed, Grandfather Irby was crafty beyond his years. After he and Mary, then sixteen, were married on a Saturday evening in 1947, they couldn't afford a real honeymoon. So after their wedding ceremony, they went to their new little home as man and wife. Some of my grandmother's nieces and nephews and cousins showed up. (The day she was born, Mary was already an aunt many, many times over because she's the baby of ten.) Anyway, they all came over to Irby and Mary's house, and they stayed, and they stayed, and they stayed. Pretty soon (or not so soon) it had gotten quite late. All of a sudden, Grandfather Irby got just sick as a dog—so sick to his stomach that he was absolutely writhing and groaning in sheer agony. (No, it couldn't have been my grandmother's cooking; she hadn't even had a chance to cook yet!)

Well, all of the nieces and nephews and

Sweet Potatoes with Topping

■ BY MARY MANDRELL

3	cups cooked and mashed sweet potatoes
$1^{1}/_{2}$	cups sugar
2	eggs
1	teaspoon vanilla extract
$^{1}/_{2}$	cup milk
$^{1}/_{3}$	cup margarine, softened
$^{2}/_{3}$	cup firmly packed light brown sugar
$^{1}/_{3}$	cup all-purpose flour
1	cup chopped pecans

In a bowl mix potatoes, sugar, eggs, vanilla, and milk, and pour into a large casserole dish. In another bowl mix remaining ingredients together. Top sweet potatoes with mixture and bake in a 350° oven for 30 minutes.

SERVINGS: 6

cousins finally decided it was time they all hugged and said their good-byes in order to leave poor Mary to tend to her violently ill husband. But what do you know? . . . As soon as the door closed behind the last guest, an amazing thing happened: Irby's illness was instantly cured!

The next morning my grandfather got up and decided to make a special pancake breakfast for his new bride. What better way, he thought, to break in some of the brand new pots and pans they acquired for their new home together. Irby cooked the pancakes on one side and was ready to flip them when—you guessed it—he found that they were sticking like glue to the new pans. It was time to improvise—and fast. Grandfather Irby "scrambled" to decide what to do, and like the good cook he wasn't, decided to "scramble" the pancakes. (Yes, for those of you keeping

Bride and groom: Mary Ellen McGill and Irby Matthew Mandrell.

Tomato Soup

■ BY MARY MANDRELL

8	ounces canned tomatoes, mashed
	Salt and pepper
½	teaspoon baking soda
½	cup whole milk

In a saucepan heat the tomatoes to the boiling point. Add salt and pepper to taste. While stirring, add soda and milk. (The soup should foam.) When the foaming peaks, remove from heat. Stir well and serve.

SERVINGS: 1

score at home, Scrambled Pancakes has the distinction of being, for better or for worse, officially our oldest family recipe.)

Fortunately, this fiasco occurred on Sunday morning, and Mary and Irby escaped the breakfast by going to church. Lots of prayers no doubt were said that day. We're not saying what prayers, but to this day, Irby has never made pancakes again. Or just maybe, *somebody* has made a solemn vow, and he's sticking to it (like pancakes).

These days it's my father, Ken, who is the pancake specialist. (See his technique for peanut butter pancakes in "Home Cooking is Best," page 67.)

———◆———

Mom and Dad have some interesting newlywed sagas of their own. They were married ten days before Mom graduated from high school in 1967. They figured that would allow them

Mary and Irby (1959).

Simple Chinese Chicken

■ BY MATT DUDNEY

1	cup sliced chicken
	Oil
1	carrot, sliced
2	stalks celery, sliced
1	red bell pepper, sliced
1	green bell pepper, sliced
1	can water chestnuts, drained
2	teaspoons soy sauce
1	pinch ground ginger
1	teaspoon cornstarch
3	tablespoons water
4	servings white rice

In a skillet sauté chicken in oil, adding vegetables halfway through cooking. Add soy sauce and ginger and continue to cook. Mix cornstarch in water and add when chicken is thoroughly cooked. (The cornstarch will thicken sauce; add more water if necessary.) Stir well and serve over rice.

SERVINGS: 4

two weeks together before Mom went to Vietnam (on a tour) to entertain the troops with the Mandrell Family Band. Meanwhile, my dad, a 26-year-old Navy pilot, was sent to Washington state.

When Mom finished her four-month tour, she assumed her days of performing music were over. The rest of the Mandrell family moved from California to Tennessee, while Mom, of course, went to Washington to join Dad, who was stationed at Whidbey Island. "Ken had found us an adorable little house to rent," Mom remembers. "It was really more like a summer house, but for us it was to be our year-round house, because even with hazardous-duty pay and flight pay, Ken still made only about $650 a month, and we had to watch our budget. But it was an adorable house. I know it was a very wonderful thing that Ken did, because it was all overgrown around the house, and he mowed the yard, and he cleaned, and he did all that he could inside to make it look as pretty as possible before I arrived."

Mom fondly remembers the delightfully rustic and sparse furnishings, combined with the glorious view of the shoreline and lovely bay, which they could see through the house's giant windows. (They seemed almost as large as the house itself.)

Hawaiian Shrimp Stir-Fry

■ BY MATT DUDNEY

1   5½ oz. can water chestnuts, drained and sliced
2   stalks celery, sliced
1   carrot, sliced
1   red bell pepper, sliced
1   green bell pepper, sliced
2   pounds shrimp, peeled and deveined
    Olive oil
1   tablespoon honey
1   10 oz. can pineapple chunks in juice
1   pinch garlic powder
1   teaspoon sesame seeds

In a large skillet sauté vegetables and shrimp in olive oil until shrimp is pink. Add honey, drained pineapple, garlic powder, and three tablespoons of the pineapple juice. Sauté for one minute. Serve over white rice and top with sesame seeds.

SERVINGS: 6

Soon Mom had the inside of the house looking as nice as the view outside. "There was a dresser with a mirror on it that was sitting next to the table in the dining room, and I immediately commenced telling Ken, 'Take this mirror off and drop it down behind the dresser and then it will just look like a nice buffet table instead of a dresser.' I was just blending my 'excellent, wifely talent' to make this home look gorgeous," Mom chuckles.

My parents' first kitchen was particularly interesting. Take the refrigerator-stove combination, for instance. "Have you ever heard of such a thing?" Mom asks. Nobody to this day has ever heard of such a thing, but sure enough, Mom and Dad's first refrigerator was about waist high and had three stove eyes on top.

There was, however, no oven, but Dad had a toaster oven left over from his bachelor days, and my mom used that as her first oven. "I wanted to bake even though most of what I baked came from cans," Mom recalls.

Barbara and Ken as newlyweds. She was such a proper Navy wife—check out the gloves.

"Biscuits or things like that were easy enough. The challenge with the toaster oven was dealing with something like a frozen pie. The first hurdle is adjusting the cooking temperature and time to allow for the fact that the toaster's door won't close because the pie is too big. Then you have to keep turning the pie in the oven to cook each section. You just keep turning it—cooking basically a third of the pie at a time. I remember that being both challenging and wonderful at the same time."

Mom adds, "I loved being a newlywed. I had a plastic record player that I paid less than forty dollars for at Sears. I had two record albums, one was Aretha Franklin with 'Respect' on it, and the other was Wes Montgomery's 'A Day in the Life.' I would do my housework and play those records. Then I figured out that I could take a patch cord and run the record player through my Standel amplifier, which I still owned. I could really blast it loud as I tried to clean and cook and plan what I wanted to do for dinner and wash the clothes and all those other wifely things."

One feature of the little house that my parents loved was the fireplace. "It was so romantic," Mom recalls. "And because money was so short, I found that I could take this little old abandoned red wagon that was in the neighborhood and pull it with me to collect driftwood from the

Barbara and Ken at their wedding reception.

Barbara's Steak Marinade

One day Mom decided to splurge and make a steak dinner. When she went to the grocery store, she realized that she couldn't tell one cut of meat from the other. For economy, she bought a round steak. "It looked good to me and it was what we could afford," she recalls. She prepared the meal and anxiously awaited her new husband's arrival. She had broiled the steaks to well-done, as that was how they both ate beef at the time. When they sat down to dinner and prepared to take their first bites, they discovered that the meat was so tough they couldn't cut it. Mom was quite upset, as any eighteen-year-old trying to make a nice meal for her new husband would be. Dad found out that his new bride had a lot to learn about cooking.

Today, Mom makes a great steak. She uses a delicious marinade to soften and flavor it, and Dad and I are a lot less likely to lose a tooth.

1	cup Worcestershire sauce
⅔	cup soy sauce
1	tablespoon ground ginger

Any amount can be made, but remember to use one-third less soy sauce than Worcestershire sauce. Mix ingredients and marinate steak for at least two hours before cooking.

SERVINGS: 4

shore, and then I could burn that wood in my fireplace. It would burn really pretty colors. (I found out later that you're not supposed to do that.)"

Mom also remembers that for "the first week, maybe even two weeks," it was really fun cleaning their house and cooking the meals, but then it got really old, really fast. Dad loves to tell people that when they were first married, my mom said, "You know this marriage thing is not all it's cracked up to be because I've got to wash the clothes, I've got to make the beds, I've got to cook the dinners, I've got to sweep the floors, and then I just turn around and a couple of weeks later I've got to do it all over again." Mom admits now, "I *was* pretty much that bad."

My parents recall the lean days of living on a strict budget during their early years of marriage. There were times when they would be grocery shopping. Mom would be filling the cart, and then Dad, whose mind is like a mainframe computer when it comes to numbers, would tell her that she'd just gone over their budget and they'd have to choose which items to keep and which ones to put back. Sometimes it was a choice of something as basic as a half-gallon of milk or a can of beans. But that kind of experience makes you even more thankful for every meal you have.

———◆———

Aunt Irlene married Rob Pincus, whose mother knows how to make Italian food—the real stuff, not what you get from that chef in a can. Irlene wanted to please Rob

Scalloped Potatoes

■ BY LOUISE MANDRELL

⅓ cup butter
⅓ cup all-purpose flour
2½ cups milk
3 cups shredded sharp Cheddar cheese
1½ teaspoons salt
1 teaspoon pepper
½ teaspoon dry mustard
6 medium potatoes, peeled and sliced
2 onions, sliced and separated
Paprika

In a saucepan over low heat, melt butter, adding flour gradually while mixing. Slowly add milk and simmer until thick and bubbly. Stir in cheese, salt, mustard, and pepper. Layer in a large casserole dish as follows: sauce, potato, and onion. Finish with the sauce. Dust top with paprika. Bake 60 to 90 minutes in a 375° oven.

SERVINGS: 6

by preparing a special Valentine's Day dinner, so she called his mother and got a recipe for stromboli, a calzone-like sandwich of meat and cheese.

From a creativity standpoint, Irlene outdid herself. She formed the stromboli in the shape of a heart. Usually it's a good thing to be creative. But experienced cooks know not to try new things when you have just one shot at getting it right, as in a holiday setting or a meal for guests. Irlene learned the hard way. The heart didn't look right so she tried to perform a little surgery by massaging it into a better heart shape with her hands. In the end, the attacked heart looked more like a stressed liver.

The table was set and the candles lit when Rob sat down for the romantic dinner. Irlene brought out the entrée and first comment was, "You made me meat loaf for Valentine's Day?" She explained that it was not meat loaf but stromboli, and even better, it was his mother's recipe. Oh, well, sure, now that you mention it, *of course* that was Mother Pincus's stromboli. What *could* Rob have been thinking! (He obviously hadn't been around wily Grandfather Irby enough yet.) Anyway, Irlene and Rob settled down to eat the unusual-looking, but tasty, stromboli. I've included in this chapter Irlene's recipe for stromboli in its traditional shape that I hope will win *your* heart.

———◆———

Aunt Louise's story is one of deception. While she was dating her husband, John

Leigh Ann's Chocolate Chess Pie

Even if your "significant other" doesn't cook much, her mother might. My girlfriend's mother is a wonderful cook, and she gave this recipe to Leigh Ann—the only thing I know she can make.

1½	cups sugar
3	tablespoons cocoa
5	ounces evaporated milk
1	teaspoon vanilla extract
2	eggs, beaten
¼	cup softened margarine
1	uncooked pie shell

In a bowl mix sugar and cocoa together. Mix in remaining ingredients (except pie shell). Mix until smooth and pour into pie shell. Bake in a 350° oven for 45 minutes. Allow to cool and serve.

SERVINGS: 8

Use my grandmother's pie crust recipe on page 44 to make a pie people won't stop talking about.

Matt's White Bread

After years of deception and premade frozen-dough bread, Aunt Louise finally broke down and learned to make homemade bread. She doesn't do it very often, because freezer dough is so convenient, but when she does make it from scratch, she uses this delicious recipe.

1   teaspoon sugar
1¼   cups warm water
1   package active dry yeast
3   tablespoons butter
1   cup milk
6   cups all-purpose flour*
2   tablespoons sugar
2   teaspoons salt

*You'll want the dough to be soft but not too sticky. Start with 5½ cups of flour, but add more during the kneading process if necessary.

In a small bowl dissolve one teaspoon sugar in one-half cup of water, adding yeast at the end. In a saucepan melt butter in milk, then allow to return to room temperature. Sift flour and two tablespoons sugar with salt. Add the liquid ingredients and knead the dough until soft. In a flour-lined bowl allow the dough to rise until double in size. Be sure to cover the bowl with a damp cloth.

Starting by pressing down the center of the dough, knead until it returns to its original size. Repeat the rising process. After dough has risen for the second time, about 1½ hours, split and place in two greased loaf pans, about 8½ by 5½ inches, and allow to rise again. Bake in a 400° oven for 30 to 45 minutes, depending on the oven.

SERVINGS: 16

Bride and groom: Louise Mandrell and John Haywood with Louise's maid of honor, her daughter Nicole.

Haywood (who is also a good cook, by the way), she often prepared elaborate meals to please him. These dinners always included freshly baked bread. John was impressed that she would go to the trouble of making bread for him every time she cooked him dinner.

What John didn't know was that she was buying bread dough from the freezer section of the grocery store. John would praise her so often for her troubles that she couldn't bring herself to admit that she wasn't really making homemade bread at all.

Louise got away with this deception for a long time until, as a couple, they hosted dinner guests. Louise prepared the meal and her frozen-dough bread. Dinner was going well and Louise received many compliments. Eventually, one of the guests asked, "Is this the bread that you buy as dough and bake it yourself? This stuff is great and a wonderful time saver." Louise finally told the truth. She had some explaining to do to John.

Irlene and her husband, Rob Pincus.

Irlene's Stromboli

1	loaf frozen bread dough, thawed
	Oil
1½	teaspoons leaf oregano
4	slices American cheese
4	ounces mozzarella cheese, grated
¼	pound ham, sliced
¼	pound hard salami, sliced
¼	pound pepperoni sausage, sliced

Allow dough to rise at room temperature. Preheat oven to 375°. Roll dough into a large rectangle. Spread one tablespoon of oil over dough and sprinkle with one teaspoon of oregano. Layer with cheese and meat, leaving the edges uncovered. Roll ends together to form a loaf. Seal ends by squeezing or folding together. Place on a cookie sheet covered with foil and sprayed with nonstick oil. Rub top of loaf with oil and sprinkle with remaining oregano. Bake for 45 minutes or until golden brown (turning once to allow even baking). Allow to cool for 15 minutes before slicing.

SERVINGS: 6

Matthew and longtime girlfriend, Leigh Ann McCluskey.

Fortunately, John has a good sense of humor. He thought the whole thing was a good joke and to this day, he still teases her about her bread.

———◆———

They say the way to a man's heart is through his stomach. Well, it can work both ways. I met my girlfriend through a mutual friend who dropped out of a three-person evening out. We continued our date and went to the opening of a new dance club and restaurant. I offered to cook dinner for our third date and she accepted. I wanted to cook something special but nothing too time-consuming. She had told me that she liked Chinese food. That was good news to me, because I love to cook Asian food.

With Asian dishes, you prepare your ingredients first and then line them up for quick cooking. I did the prep work and waited for her to arrive. After she arrived, we talked while I cooked. We were both a little nervous, but she was still impressed. She later confessed that she was expecting something not quite as delicious. I always said that I learned to cook because it impressed girls, and because it worked so well, I have included a few Asian recipes in this chapter for those prenewlywed guys "trying to impress."

———◆———

As all young families do, we've had some zany moments in our days as newlyweds and young loves. And, sure, there are often trying times. But my mom has some words of experience for newlyweds who might be reading this book. (Maybe this is even their first cookbook as a married couple!)

"When Ken and I were engaged and got married, I thought, 'This is going to be so wonderful just to be Mrs. Kenneth L. Dudney and just clean my house and cook and be Susie Homemaker.' But it's just not that simple. And for the man, or even if you're a working wife, it's even heavier. But the main thing is that now you've got someone else to consider. There's always this other person's needs to consider. When you're on your own, you can act on just what you think. You can

ask yourself, 'What do I want to do? How do I want to do this? How do I want to look? What do I want to buy? What movie do I want to see? What television show do I want to watch tonight?' But when you become a couple, your life's not just you anymore. Now you have two parts—you and your spouse. You always have to consider the other person, and that's not always fun."

———◆———

Being able to sit down with your family for a nice meal is one of life's great, simple pleasures. And doing so is built on love and devotion. And yes, at the same time, part of the building process is knowing how to feign a stomach illness to get rid of relatives, or figuring out the proper method for rotating pies in a toaster oven, or trying to make heart-shaped meals, or keeping your secret dough in the freezer. It's the little things that start with young loves and newlyweds that often grow into the key ingredients of meaningful family traditions.

28· **1882**

MILES
TO
NORTH POLE

1977

Jaime, Santa, and Matt.

CHAPTER 2

The Mandrell Family Christmas

One of our family's most special traditions is Christmas. The season is such an important family time to us that we usually end up having two celebrations and family gatherings. One gathering is the traditional, sacred, Christmas celebration on December 25th, which is when we usually celebrate with our individual families.

However, because of the separate careers and busy lives of each of the three sisters and their families, we have found it necessary in our lives to have a Mandrell Family Christmas to bring us all back together.

Mom says, "I don't remember when there wasn't a Mandrell Family Christmas, other than the first year Ken and I were in Washington. In fact, we couldn't afford even to call my parents that Christmas. Every two or three months had to be our custom for long-distance phone calls back in those days."

But ever since then, we look weeks in advance at each other's schedules and we find a tentative date when all of us can get together. If something comes along and we have to change the date, then we all go back to the calendars and search for a date that works. It doesn't matter that it's not December 25th. It is the highest priority for all of us to find a date that works; Mom has simply made it a Mandrell Family mandate. Some years we've had to pick a date as early as November for Mandrell Family Christmas, because our families absolutely must be together.

Because of the separate careers and busy lives of each of the three sisters and their families, we have found it necessary in our lives to have a Mandrell Family Christmas.

As much as possible, our families take turns hosting the Mandrell Family Christmas, but we all pitch in help with the preparations and the cooking. It doesn't matter if, in a particular year, we each cook dishes in our separate kitchens and take them to the home of the host; or if one person does most of the preparation; or if a cafeteria prepares the food and we just pick it up and bring it home. The important thing is that we all get to be together.

When it comes to Christmas itself, the Dudney family has three traditions: We spend a tremendous amount of time eating, we take photographs, and we laugh a lot. Our rationale is that our family doesn't spend much time together during the year, so we set aside time to bring the clan together in Aspen, Colorado. As with the larger Mandrell Family Christmas, the target date for converging on Aspen changes several times over the year because of schedule conflicts. Thankfully, it has always worked out that we have

Christmas Turkey

■ BY MATT DUDNEY

1	18+ pound turkey, rinsed well, giblets removed
	Olive oil
2	lemons
½	cup fresh oregano
½	cup fresh basil
3	sprigs fresh rosemary
½	cup fresh thyme
2	cloves fresh garlic
1	cup butter
	Paprika
	Salt and white pepper

Clean the turkey well with water. Using your hands, carefully separate the skin from the breast meat. (Do not remove the skin, just pull it away from the meat. You will be creating a pocket between the skin and the breast meat.) Rub the breast meat with oil and the juice from two lemons. Place lemon rinds in the cavity of the turkey.

Pull the leaves from one-half of the fresh herbs and place them on top of the turkey breast in between the pocket of skin. Place remaining herbs and garlic in the cavity of the bird, along with the butter. Rub oil over entire bird and sprinkle with paprika, salt, and pepper.

Line a roasting pan that is at least four inches deep with aluminum foil. (Use lots of foil, for you will be using the excess to cover the top of the bird before it goes into the oven.) Place turkey in roasting pan and fill with 1½ to 2 inches of water. Close foil and bake in a 350° oven until the internal temperature of the breast reaches 165° or the leg joint reaches a temperature of 180°. (You will want to baste the turkey often.)

I personally like to cook my turkey to 165° in the leg joint. I then carve it and place it in a casserole dish covering it with its own juices for storage overnight in the refrigerator. When you reheat the turkey in the oven the next day, it finishes cooking and stays very juicy. Remember to save the basting for the gravy.

SERVINGS: AT LEAST 12

been able to spend this one day together as a family.

We attend church services on Christmas Eve and sing Christmas carols while we're there, but otherwise, we don't spend a lot of time singing at home. Over the years we've become good friends with the minister and his wife. In fact, he is also the trailmaster when Mom, Dad, and Nathan go horseback riding in the summer.

On Christmas day, the tradition is to get up around 8:30 A.M. As the head elf in charge of putting the gifts out, Mom is up long before that. We don't make a big breakfast,

The Dudney family at dinner with their preacher Edgell Pyle and his wife Marty of the Snowmass Chapel in Aspen, Colorado.

Turkey Gravy

■ BY MATT DUDNEY

Basting liquid from cooked turkey
Roux (see recipe page 155)
Shredded turkey
Cajun seasoning

Strain the basting into a pan and set aside. Make a roux, about one cup's worth, and add liquid to the roux while whisking constantly. Mix shredded turkey pieces into the gravy and simmer for about ten minutes. Serve hot. Add a dash of Cajun seasoning to the gravy to really brighten up the flavor.

SERVINGS: 12

Virginia Terry's Alabama Turkey

■ BY BARBARA MANDRELL

When my husband, Ken, was shipped out to serve on the USS Independence, I moved to Tennessee for nine months. I did not have enough income to live on my own, so I stayed with my musician friends Gordon and Virginia Terry. Gordon was a talented singer and fiddle and guitar player—a wonderful entertainer. That year I spent Thanksgiving with them, and Virginia made this delicious turkey. I'm telling you that woman can cook. She's the epitome of great cooks. At the time I lived with them, if I hadn't been just nineteen years old with a high metabolism, I would have gained 6,000 pounds. They had a great tradition, which I guess is Southern, of having this big meal with all these wonderful vegetables, meats, and breads, and then all the desserts. It was the kind of meal that most of us only cook on Thanksgiving and Christmas, but it was just an everyday meal for them. She gave me the turkey recipe from that day, and now I'm passing it along to you.

1	**whole turkey, rinsed and drained**
	Margarine
	Salt
	Lemon pepper
1	**pound sliced bacon**

Rub inside and outside of bird with margarine. Sprinkle with salt and lemon pepper inside and out. Cover entire bird with bacon, place in a roasting pan, and cover with aluminum foil. Cook turkey in a 350° oven to an internal temperature of 180° at the leg joint. Remove bacon and brown. The bacon will baste the bird and leave a wonderful flavor.

SERVINGS: 10

Irby loves Christmas. Here he is opening presents at the Mandrell Family Christmas, 1998.

but instead just enjoy donuts and fresh-squeezed orange juice. We eat light in preparation for Christmas dinner around 3:00 P.M.

———◆———

One year, Mom was preparing Christmas dinner, as was the family tradition. She put the turkey in the oven and prepared the sweet potatoes for roasting. She peeled some more potatoes and put them in a covered pot with water, ready to be boiled and mashed. She added green beans to a pot with a few slices of bacon in it, and then sprinkled it all with salt,

Mary opening presents during the Mandrell Family Christmas, 1996.

Turkey Stuffing

■ BY MATT DUDNEY

In addition to the turkey, I sometimes make a few side dishes for Christmas dinner. Most of the time, my family loves the dishes I prepare. But the first time I prepared this stuffing, my grandfather Irby wasn't very pleased with it: He said it needed more sage. The next time I made it, my grandfather approved. I must've added at least double the amount of sage! This recipe is not very fancy but it is traditional to Southern tastes.

2	carrots, chopped
3	stalks celery, chopped
1	cup butter
8	cups breadcrumbs
1	teaspoon salt
½	teaspoon white pepper
1	teaspoon ground sage
½	teaspoon ground thyme
½	teaspoon garlic powder
2	eggs, beaten
	Turkey stock

In a large skillet sauté carrot and celery pieces in butter until slightly soft. Mix all ingredients together, except the eggs and turkey stock. Mix beaten eggs into breadcrumb mixture and add turkey stock until you reach desired consistency. (Remember, some of the liquid will evaporate during baking.) Place in a large casserole dish and bake in a 350° oven for 30 minutes or until lightly browned on top.

SERVINGS: 8

Italian Stuffing

■ BY MATT DUDNEY

1	stalk celery, chopped
1	carrot, chopped
1	green bell pepper, chopped
1	red bell pepper, chopped
1	cup thickly sliced button mushrooms
1	cup butter
8	cups breadcrumbs
1	cup Italian sausage, cooked and cubed
1	tablespoon fresh basil
1	tablespoon fresh oregano
1	tablespoon garlic powder
1	egg, beaten

In a large saucepan, sauté vegetables in butter. Mix in breadcrumbs, adding all other ingredients. Place in a large casserole dish and bake in a 375° oven for about 30 minutes until lightly browned on top.

SERVINGS: 8

Homemade Cranberry Sauce

■ BY MATT DUDNEY

Our family usually eats canned cranberry sauce because it's easier, but if you can get fresh cranberries, you have to try this recipe.

12	ounces fresh cranberries, washed
1/2	cup apple juice
1 1/2	cups water
1 1/4	cups sugar
1/4	teaspoon salt
1/4	teaspoon ground cinnamon
1/4	teaspoon ground cloves

Place ingredients in a saucepan and stir over medium-high heat until a boil is reached. Reduce heat to a simmer and continue to cook, stirring until the liquid has thickened and the cranberries have split. Remove from heat and allow to cool before serving.

SERVINGS: 8

pepper, and sugar. Then, she chopped the fruit for the fruit salad. So far her day was uneventful. (Susie Homemaker would have been proud.)

Meanwhile, the rest of us were on the mountain skiing. When we came home, we were immediately struck by a terrible smell. We ran upstairs to look around. Perhaps the dog had left us a surprise on the floor. To our dismay, however, the stench was coming from the oven. When we finally found Mom, she didn't know why we were so concerned. She had been in the house and around that smell all day. She hadn't noticed how bad it was.

That's when I made the bold move of opening the oven door. The awful smell filled the room and became even more putrid. It turned out that the turkey had spoiled and there had been no way to tell until it began cooking. When Mom realized what had happened, she was naturally quite upset, because she had worked so hard getting everything ready.

Dad and I sprang into action. Dad went to the store to buy another turkey and I took

Louise's Holiday Greeter

Christmas is one of my favorite holidays—so much so that I dedicate two months to Christmas at my music theater in Pigeon Forge. As a show-biz star, I often find myself doing as much entertaining off the stage as I do on it. I love to throw Christmas parties, and I often make this drink to welcome guests into my house. They can smell its cinnamon aroma as soon as they walk in the front door.

It's a warm, friendly drink, and it gives people that special feeling that they're coming home again, or that someone's busy baking in the kitchen during the holidays.

4	*cups boiling water*
4	*bags orange-mango tea*
1	*quart apple juice*
1	*quart cranberry juice*
1	*cup sugar*
2	*oranges*
1/4	*cup whole cloves*
6	*sticks cinnamon*

Pour boiling water over tea bags and steep for ten minutes. Combine tea, juices, and sugar in a large saucepan; bring to a boil. While punch is heating, stud oranges with cloves (you may need to poke holes in the oranges). Place oranges and cinnamon sticks into punch at the boiling point and remove from heat. Serve hot with a lemon or lime slice and half a stick of cinnamon.

SERVINGS: 12

Coconut Cake

■ BY LOUISE MANDRELL

My daughter, Nicole, bakes a birthday cake for the Baby Jesus, just like my sister's children—only she makes hers from scratch. I used this recipe to teach her how to bake. Sometimes Nicole adds a miniature baby doll and puts it in the middle of the coconut. . . . She thinks of the cake as a manger and the brown coconut as the hay.

3½	cups all-purpose flour
4½	teaspoons baking powder
1	teaspoon salt
1	cup butter-flavored shortening
2¼	cups sugar
8	large egg whites
1	cup whole milk
¼	teaspoon almond extract
2	teaspoons vanilla extract

In a bowl sift flour, baking powder, and salt together and set aside. In another bowl cream the shortening until light and fluffy, adding sugar gradually. Beat in one egg white at a time until all are incorporated. Add one-third of the dry ingredients, then one-half cup of milk, repeat, and finish by adding the last of the dry ingredients. Incorporate almond and vanilla extracts. Beat for two minutes. Divide the dough into three greased 9-inch cake pans and bake in a 350° oven for 30 minutes.

SERVINGS: 8

White Boiled Coconut Cake Frosting

■ BY LOUISE MANDRELL

3	cups sugar
¾	cup water
¼	cup light corn syrup
4	egg whites, beaten
⅔	cup confectioners' sugar
1	teaspoon vanilla extract
½	teaspoon almond extract
1	bag shredded coconut

In a saucepan dissolve the sugar in water; add corn syrup, and boil to soft ball stage (238°). Pour cooked syrup in a thin stream over the beaten egg whites while beating. Continue to beat until desired consistency. Add confectioners' sugar and beat until smooth. Add flavorings. Ice the layers and outside of a cake. With your hand, press coconut into the icing. Chill and serve.

SERVINGS: 8

that horrible, smelly thing outside and disposed of it. Dad returned with a new turkey and several cans of air freshener. He took care of the smell, and I took care of the bird. In the end, Christmas dinner turned out fine. Mom even said she had never tasted a better turkey. To this day, I cook the turkey and make the gravy every Christmas.

———◆———

Christmas Day itself is an extra-special time for Mom because December 25th is also her birthday. "People ask me all the time what it's like to have my birthday on Christmas," Mom says. "I'm a Christian so it's a real privilege to be born on a day that we celebrate as Jesus's birthday. To be born on that day is wonderful."

Mom does admit, however, that at a very young age, she began sorting the Christmas gifts and birthday gifts that she received into separate piles. "I would put my birthday gifts on top of the TV or over on a table, not under the tree. I was born around 3 o'clock in the afternoon, so we would celebrate my birthday in the afternoon. Every year I'd make an announcement to the effect, 'Okay, this is my time, and if you didn't get me a birthday gift, that's fine. But the Christmas gifts aren't

Nathan with his birthday cake for Baby Jesus.

opened as part of my birthday celebration.' As a Christmas birthday child, you have to let the rules be known," Mom laughs. (By the way, for those who might be wondering, the rule is still enforced.)

Dad, Nathan, Jaime, and Matt celebrating Barbara's birthday.

Bread Pudding

■ BY MATT DUDNEY

1½ cups bread cubes
2 cups heavy cream
1 cup milk, scalded
2 eggs
½ cup sugar
¼ teaspoon salt
½ teaspoon ground cinnamon
¼ teaspoon grated nutmeg
½ cup seedless raisins*

Soak bread in cream and milk for one-half hour. In a bowl, beat the eggs, gradually adding the sugar. Beat in salt, cinnamon, and nutmeg. Stir in the raisins and combine egg mixture with bread. Pour into a large casserole dish and set in a pan of hot water. Bake in a 350° oven for 45 to 50 minutes.

SERVINGS: 6

Be creative; you may want to use dried cranberries or figs in place of or in addition to the raisins.

Mom has her children bake two birthday cakes for Christmas Day. One is for her birthday and the other is for Baby Jesus. We use cake mix to make the cakes, but we get creative when we decorate. Sometimes we spell out their names with candy, sometimes with icing, and one year my brother Nathan used mini-marshmallows to spell out, "Happy Birthday, Jesus." The fun of making His cake also helps to remind us why we are celebrating Christmas.

Mom's cake is always chocolate, and the family saves it for a few hours after we've finished the obligatory Christmas pumpkin pie. That way we can make her birthday a separate event. As a result, we do even more eating than most families on Christmas day.

Still, Mom doesn't dictate *all* the terms of her birthday celebrations. Take Christmas 1998. Mom had lain down to take a nap after dinner. After a while there came a knock at her bedroom door. I came in and handed her this little card in an envelope. She opened it. (It was a little children's invitation to a birthday party.) I asked her if she was ready to go into the living room. I blindfolded her with a dish towel and guided her toward the kitchen instead. When I pulled the towel off, the whole area had been decorated with crepe paper, paper hats and napkins, and all kinds of birthday goodies—all while Mom was napping.

Mom recalls the occasion with glee. "My three children and my husband gave me my little surprise birthday party in the kitchen on Christmas evening, and they drank a toast to me and gave me the most clever cake. It was exactly the cake I wanted— chocolate cake with rich chocolate icing and nuts on it and all. Now, I won't tell you what

Pecan Pie

■ BY MATT DUDNEY

3	eggs, beaten
1	cup dark corn syrup
1	cup sugar
1	teaspoon vanilla extract
1	cup pecans
1	9-inch pie crust, unbaked

In a bowl combine all ingredients and pour into unbaked pie shell. Bake in a 325° oven for one hour.

SERVINGS: 6

I always make this with my grandmother's homemade pie crust recipe (see page 44)

Mary's Pumpkin Pie

The only downside to the great food at Christmas is that we all gain about five pounds and can never figure out why. Desserts? Who's counting! Pumpkin pie has to be one of the things we simply can't resist. My grandmother makes one of the best you'll ever put in your mouth. Dad won't let her into the house for Mandrell Family Christmas or Thanksgiving if she doesn't have at least two pies in-hand.

1	15 oz. can pumpkin
¾	cup sugar
1	teaspoon ground cinnamon
½	teaspoon ground ginger
¼	teaspoon ground cloves
¼	teaspoon ground nutmeg
2	eggs
1½	cups evaporated milk
1	pie crust (9-inch), unbaked*

Mix the pumpkin with the sugar, cinnamon, ginger, cloves, and nutmeg. Beat eggs in a separate bowl and slowly combine with the pumpkin mixture, adding the evaporated milk last. Pour filling into the pie shell and bake in a 425° oven for 15 minutes. Reduce temperature to 350° and continue baking for 40 to 45 minutes.

There's no better way to top off the holiday season than with a piece (or two or three!) of my grandmother's pumpkin pie.

*I like to bake my pie shell for four to five minutes before adding my filling.

Mary's Homemade Pie Crust

2	cups all-purpose flour
1	teaspoon salt
¾	cup olive oil
¼	cup evaporated milk*

In a bowl sift flour and salt together. Mix the oil and milk together and add to flour mixture. Mix dough and separate into two portions, saving the larger portion for the bottom. Place dough between two pieces of wax paper and roll out into a round. Repeat with the remaining dough.

SERVINGS: 2

*For a firmer crust use more milk; for a more flaky crust use less milk.

birthday that was . . . but the party sure was *nifty.*"

———◆———

One year my grandparents, Mary and Irby, spent Christmas with us in Aspen, and they brought their dogs, Killer and Dinky. When they arrived, the Christmas spirit was complete. Presents were piled beneath the Christmas tree, snow was falling outside, and the house smelled of cinnamon. All of us were fully in the Christmas spirit.

Mom always buys presents for the family dogs, and that year she bought gifts for Killer and Dinky

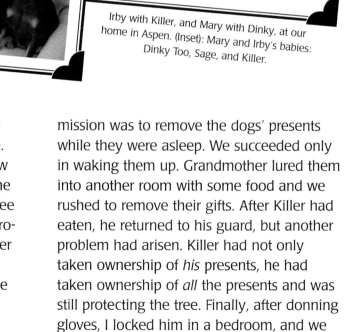

Irby with Killer, and Mary with Dinky, at our home in Aspen. (Inset): Mary and Irby's babies: Dinky Too, Sage, and Killer.

Too. She showed the dogs their wrapped presents and placed them under the tree. This is where she made her mistake. Now that Killer knew where his present was, he assumed that anyone approaching the tree was after his gift. He guarded the tree ferociously. It was funny at first, because Killer doesn't realize that he's a *miniature* pinscher. (He seems to think he's the full-size version.) No one, not even master Irby, could get near that tree.

Christmas morning came and our main mission was to remove the dogs' presents while they were asleep. We succeeded only in waking them up. Grandmother lured them into another room with some food and we rushed to remove their gifts. After Killer had eaten, he returned to his guard, but another problem had arisen. Killer had not only taken ownership of *his* presents, he had taken ownership of *all* the presents and was still protecting the tree. Finally, after donning gloves, I locked him in a bedroom, and we opened our gifts in peace.

The whole family on skis, 1988.

Aspen
Our Second Home

Our connection with Aspen began in 1975 when my parents went skiing there with some friends. There was a two-bedroom condominium for sale at a very reasonable price, and my parents took a chance and bought it. Money was still pretty tight back then, so it was set up as a rental property that could be used by the owners for just two weeks per year. We always chose two weeks around Christmas. Our family owned that condo until 1992. But when Nathan was old enough to walk and get into trouble, we needed more space, so we bought a house. The house is big enough for Mom and Dad to have their own bedroom and for Jaime, Nathan, and me to have our own rooms as well. The house is there for us to use whenever we like, and we generally spend a month there each summer and a couple of weeks around Christmas.

Our home in Colorado is really as much a part of our family life as our home in Tennessee. Everyone in our family has some reason that the Aspen home is his or her favorite place to get away. The house sits about 9,000 feet above sea level, and Mom and Dad love the dramatic mountain view that they wake up to each day. As Mom says, "Every day I look out that window and just think, 'Ohhhh.' It just takes my breath away. It's just a real right-in-my-face expression of how mighty God is."

The house was built with view, view, and more view. It's pretty wonderful that way. And we love the kitchen there. There's a deck off the kitchen with a gas grill, and in the summer, we put an umbrella and table out on the deck. "Eating out" that way is just marvelous. If the music festival is going on, the mountains really come alive with the music.

> **O**ur home in Colorado is really as much a part of our family life as our home in Tennessee.

*F*or a family like ours that loves to find mountains to climb, Aspen has been a source of tremendous joy for all of us. One of the real pleasures of Aspen has been that it's a refuge—a place that, even though we're surrounded by these most majestic mountains, we're able to relax and unwind. We read books, watch television, and play board games. In the winter, Nathan loves to hit the slopes with his snowboard. Jaime and I particularly enjoy skiing. In the summer, we all go horseback riding, fly-fishing, hiking, and white-water rafting, but despite all the attractions in Aspen, our family's favorite thing to do is just stay at home and cook and eat. Aspen and the surrounding area have many great restaurants, but whenever we're in town, Mom does lots of

Ralph Emery's Favorite Chili

■ BY BARBARA MANDRELL

Ralph Emery and his family have been coming to Colorado to ski for as long as I can remember. "Uncle Ralph," as my kids call him, always asks me to make this chili for him and his wife Joy. You might find it a bit spicy, but in the cold Colorado Rockies, nothing will get you warmer faster than my chili.

1	pound pinto beans, soaked and drained
2½	pounds ground beef or ground turkey
2	yellow onions, diced
1	green bell pepper, diced
2	stalks celery, diced
1	clove garlic, crushed
2	tablespoons diced pepperoncini peppers
1	8 oz. can tomato paste
¼	cup chili powder
1	tablespoon cayenne
3	1.31 oz. packages Sloppy Joe mix
2	tablespoons jalapeño juice (optional)

In a large pan cook pinto beans in water to cover. In a skillet lightly brown ground beef. Add vegetables. After vegetables soften, add pinto beans, tomato paste, and all spices and liquids. Add water if needed, and salt and pepper to taste. Cook on low heat for 45 to 60 minutes and serve.

SERVINGS: 8

cooking and entertaining. Friends from Nashville visit and they all have their favorite Barbara Mandrell dish.

———◆———

One year recently, Mom was making her famous chili for Ralph Emery and his wife Joy, when she thought it would be nice to invite Reba McEntire, Reba's husband Narvel Blackstock, and their son Shelby over to join us since they're friends of our family as well as the Emery's.

When Reba and Narvel told Mom they had eleven people with them, Mom figured, "No problem; the more the merrier. We've got a big enough

Irby, Barbara, Reba McEntire, and Narvel Blackstock in 1993.
(photo by Judy Mock)

Corn Flake Bread

■ BY MATT DUDNEY

1	*package active dry yeast*
½	*cup warm water*
½	*cup corn flake crumbs*
⅓	*cup sugar*
½	*cup vegetable shortening*
¼	*teaspoon salt*
½	*cup boiling water*
1	*egg*
3	*cups all-purpose flour*

In a small bowl dissolve yeast in warm water. In a large bowl mix corn flake crumbs, sugar, shortening, and salt. Pour boiling water over the corn flake mixture. Stir, let cool, then add yeast. Next, add egg and half of flour. Beat well. Add remaining flour and knead well. Cover and let rise until double in size. Push down. Form into two small loaves, place in buttered pans, and let rise again until the dough doubles in size. Before baking, brush tops of loaves with melted butter. Bake in a 350° oven for 30 to 35 minutes.

Notes: After first rising, dough may be punched down and placed in the refrigerator overnight, or it may be mixed and placed right in refrigerator and both risings done the second day. If refrigerated, allow to stand at room temperature for a couple of hours before proceeding.

SERVINGS: 12

Artichoke Dip

■ BY BARBARA MANDRELL

When guests come to visit, Mom always makes a tray with cheese and crackers or sets out some chips with salsa. Occasionally, she adds this arti-choke dip, which my sisters' godmother, Janice Lovvorn, gave her. It never seems to be around very long, which is a true testament to its tasti-ness. The best part of this recipe is its simplicity. I've added my versions of salsa and guacamole, too, because Mom and I have a friendly competi-tion going about whose dips are the best. I love hers and she loves mine. May the best dip win!

1	10 oz. can drained and chopped artichoke hearts
¼	cup Parmesan cheese
3	tablespoons mayonnaise

Irby hits the slopes in Aspen.

Mix ingredients together in a bowl. Place in a small casserole dish and bake at 350° for 15 minutes or until edges start to brown. For variation, you can also add crab-meat and/or jalapeños.

SERVINGS: 6

Matt's Fresh Salsa

4	tomatoes, peeled and chopped
1	large onion, chopped
2	tablespoons chopped fresh cilantro
3	tablespoons chopped jalapeños
1	tablespoon rice wine vinegar
2	tablespoons lime juice
	Salt and white pepper

In a bowl mix all ingredients and add salt and pepper to taste. Chill before serving.

SERVINGS: 8

pot to swing it." Mom had planned to make a pretty big batch of chili this year anyway. So she rolled up her sleeves and prepared chili for a total of seventeen people. Well, she got busy cooking the pinto beans two days early, because at high altitude they take more time to cook. "You just keep cooking them and finally they're done," she says smiling.

Mom had her pinto beans ready in plenty of time and she had plenty of ground beef in the freezer. When the time came to

Matt's Traditional Guacamole

3   avocados, peeled
1   tablespoon lime juice
1   teaspoon canned jalapeño pepper juice
1   teaspoon garlic powder
    Salt and pepper

In a bowl mash avocados, mixing in liquids and garlic powder. Salt and pepper to taste. Chill before serving.

SERVINGS: 8

Matt's Standard Guacamole

Here is a standard guacamole recipe, just in case you want to compare.

3   whole avocados
1   tablespoon fresh lemon juice
1   teaspoon Tabasco sauce
½   onion, minced
2   whole jalapeño peppers, seeded and chopped
1   whole fresh tomato, chopped
1   tablespoon chopped fresh cilantro*
½   teaspoon salt
½   teaspoon pepper

Peel and slice avocados. Add all liquids. Mash and add remaining ingredients. Serve as a dip with chips or crackers.

SERVINGS: 8

Substitute one tablespoon of chopped parsley and one-half teaspoon of ground coriander if fresh cilantro is not available.

start the chili, she thawed the beef and then sautéed it with some vegetables and poured it all into the pot. Voila! The amount of chili just kept growing. Worried she still wouldn't have enough, she asked Dad to stop by the grocery store and pick up some canned pinto beans. (Hey! No fair! That's cheating!)

Well, Mom drained the cans and added the beans. Now she had a lobster pot full of chili—more than enough to feed an army of hungry mountaineers. Everything was all set. Then . . . get ready . . . "ring-ring." Mom, it's Reba calling. Turns out it's gonna be just Reba, Narvel, and Shelby coming. The rest of the troops are still on the slopes.

Needless to say there was plenty of chili

Aspen Snowballs

■ BY BARBARA MANDRELL

This is one of my family's favorite Aspen recipes. It originated at a restaurant Ken and I visited in Aspen some twenty-five years ago. I started making it soon afterwards, but to this day I've made it only six times, because it's such a pain to prepare. Just imagine making a snowball out of ice cream without wearing gloves! As you can imagine, your hands get pretty cold. But my pain and suffering never go without praise. This is a delicious dish that pleases everyone, and it's really not quite as painful as I make it sound. But you really do have to love someone to want to make it for them.

Shredded coconut
Vanilla ice cream
Hot fudge

Brown the coconut lightly on a cookie sheet in a 300° oven. Mold the ice cream, using your hands, into a snowball-size ball. (Have lukewarm water running; your hands will get cold.) Roll the ice cream ball in coconut and place in the freezer. Heat the hot fudge in a stove-top double boiler or in a microwave oven. Spoon hot fudge onto a small plate and place the snowball in the center.

SERVINGS: 1

When Matthew was in high school, I made these for him and the whole football team. Everyone raved about them, so my cold hands were worth it. NO PAIN, NO GAIN!

left over for Joy, Uncle Ralph, Reba, Narvel, and Shelby to carry big bowls back with them. And we even had enough chili left to last us for many days.

◆

This happens more often than you might think. When we spend the holidays in Aspen, we always seem to have lots of leftovers. Since we know we only have a limited number of days left before we head back to Tennessee, we've started making the leftovers into new dishes that we can

Barbara serving Matthew one of her famous Aspen Snowballs in her soda fountain room.

Cream of Spinach Soup

■ BY MATT DUDNEY

1   *small shallot, minced*
2   *tablespoons butter*
2   *tablespoons all-purpose flour*
2   *pounds fresh spinach, stems removed*
2   *cups chicken stock*
2   *cups heavy cream*
   Salt and white pepper

In a skillet sauté shallot in butter until almost transparent; add flour and stir. Place in food processor. In a saucepan wilt one-half of the spinach in water with salt. Drain well and add to shallots. Add three tablespoons of chicken stock to food processor and purée. In a large saucepan bring remaining chicken stock and purée mixture to a boil. Remove from heat and add heavy cream and remaining spinach while stirring. Salt and pepper to taste and serve with bread.

SERVINGS: 4

Ken, Barbara, Matthew, Nathan, Dandy, and Chouette picking out their Christmas tree in Aspen, 1998.

Turkey Croquettes

■ BY MATT DUDNEY

5	cups cooked and shredded turkey
2	stalks celery, minced
1	onion, minced
2	eggs, beaten
1	teaspoon garlic powder
	Salt and pepper to taste
3	eggs, beaten
2	cups seasoned breadcrumbs

In a large bowl mix turkey, celery, onion, two eggs, garlic powder, salt, and pepper. Form bell-shaped croquettes from turkey mixture. Dip in egg and roll in breadcrumbs. Place on a greased baking sheet and bake in a 350° oven for 35 minutes. Serve with gravy and mashed potatoes.

SERVINGS: 6

For a tastier (but more fattening) version, bake for 20 minutes and then deep-fry until golden brown.

enjoy eating right away—something that will be at least a little different than the usual turkey sandwiches or turkey casserole. One of our favorites is turkey croquettes, served on top of mashed potatoes and drowned in turkey gravy. But Irlene has a great recipe for ham croquettes with a cheese sauce that we also enjoy. She's included her recipe in this chapter, too, to help you get through the season without hating turkey or ham for a month.

Some other dear friends of ours from Nashville that we also seem to see only in Aspen are U.S. Senator Bill Frist, his wife Karyn, and their family. (If you get the feeling the only time we see many of our Nashville friends is in Aspen, it's practically true! That's because we're all on such different schedules which take us away from Nashville during so much of the year.) We became acquainted with the Frists through

Ham Croquettes

■ BY IRLENE MANDRELL

3	tablespoons margarine
¼	cup all-purpose flour
¾	cup milk
2	cups chopped ham
1	teaspoon grated onion
	Corn flake crumbs (or bread-crumbs)
1	egg, beaten

In a saucepan melt margarine. Blend in flour and milk. Cook and stir until thick and bubbly. Remove from heat and add ham and onion. Mix well and chill for several hours. When chilled, shape into 2-inch balls. Roll in crumbs. Dip into egg and roll in crumbs again. Deep-fry for two minutes and then drain. Serve with cheese sauce (below).

SERVINGS: 4

Cheese Sauce

■ BY IRLENE MANDRELL

1	can mushroom soup
5	slices American cheese

In a saucepan bring soup to a simmer and incorporate cheese.

SERVINGS: 4

his work as one of the leading heart- and lung-transplant surgeons in the world and through Mom's celebrity softball tournament, which raises funds for the organ transplant program at Vanderbilt University Medical Center. Now, whenever Senator Frist and his

family are in Aspen, they always come to visit. And Senator Frist always requests some of my mom's famous beef stew.

———◆———

As you can tell, our family likes to warm up during the winter by eating soups and

Mister Doctor Senator Frist Stew

■ BY BARBARA MANDRELL

When Dr. Bill Frist was first elected to the U.S. Senate, Nathan, just eight years old at the time, and trying to be very correct, didn't know how to address him. When Dr. Frist finally came to visit and Nathan began to address him, it came out as "Mister Doctor Senator Frist." For years now, I've been serving Mister Doctor Senator Frist and his family this homemade stew with cornbread. They must like it, because they keep coming back. When we have a steak dinner at home, I buy three extra steaks and marinate them overnight. Then I cook them (only to rare) and use them as a base for my stew.

3   *cups carrots, in half-inch slices*
4   *marinated steaks, grilled and cubed*
5   *medium potatoes, peeled and cubed*
3   *1.31-ounce packets Sloppy Joe mix*
2   *cups celery, in one-inch slices*
2   *medium onions, in half-inch slices*
2   *cups green bell peppers, in one-inch cubes*
2   *cups broccoli, sectioned*
1   *can corn*
1   *can green beans*
1   *can green peas*
4   *cans tomato sauce*
½   *cup salsa*
1   *can tomato soup*
4   *cloves garlic, crushed*
    Salt and pepper

Place potatoes, carrots, and steak in a large stock pot. Fill with water to cover the contents and bring to a boil. Stir in the Sloppy Joe mix and reduce heat to simmer. Cover and cook for 20 minutes. Next, add remaining ingredients and top off with water. Cover and continue to cook for 45 to 90 minutes. Remember to stir gently, and reduce the temperature if anything starts to stick to the bottom of the pot.

SERVINGS: 12

Senator Frist and his wife Karyn, with Barbara and Ken.

stews, usually with fresh bread. If we're out skiing, however, we don't want to get too full, so we try to make soups that will fill us up without stuffing us. Cream soups have always been a favorite of ours, and they are actually faster and easier to make than a vegetable soup or stew. I've included in this chapter our favorite fast-and-light soup, cream of spinach. I try to make it every year,

provided we don't have extra Ralph Emery Chili or Senator Frist Beef Stew leftover.

———◆———

All of us love Aspen so much that it really is as much a home to us as Tennessee. But we also know that the time we spend in Aspen is really more like a vacation. So it's always with a little sadness that we pack up and leave Aspen—our sights set on Tennessee.

Matthew being fed by his mother. He has always loved to eat.

Home Cooking Is Best

Our family firmly believes, as Mom says, "Home is wherever my family is. That's true whether we're at Fontanel (our home in Nashville), out in Aspen, on my bus, or even out in the woods in a tent."

One of our family's greatest pleasures is sitting down together for a home-cooked meal. It's very important to focus on what's going on in everybody's lives. Supper is about the only time that we're all together at one time, so the mealtime becomes crucial for really finding out what has happened in the lives of our family members during the day.

It's always a pleasure when Mom cooks for us because she puts so much love into what she prepares. We didn't always have her cooking growing up, especially when she was on the road. Before Jaime and Nathan were born, Dad and I would fend for ourselves when Mom was away. It wouldn't be anything fancy—just grilled cheese sandwiches, hot

> **One of our family's greatest pleasures is sitting down together for a home-cooked meal. It's very important to focus on what's going on in everybody's lives.**

dogs with beans, hamburgers, and other "bachelor" food—but it was always fun.

Today, Miss Glenda, the "true lady of the house," as Mom calls her, prepares meals for Dad and Nathan when Mom is out of town. Jaime lives in New York and I no longer live in the house, but when Jaime and I come to supper, Mom always reclaims the kitchen and cooks a meal for us all.

Aunt Louise and Aunt Irlene are also wonderful cooks, who happen to have cooking husbands as well. Rob, Irlene's husband, makes tasty Italian dishes that he learned from his mother. John, Louise's husband, likes to hunt and makes quail and dove dishes. While Rob and John have their specialties, they are probably even happier when they get to enjoy their wives' delicious cooking.

No matter who's cooking, our motto is: Have a good time in the kitchen, and while you're there, think about how much your family will enjoy the food that you make for them!

Often it's hard to look forward to preparing a weeknight dinner, especially if both parents in your household work. Our family is no different. The evening meal should be a time of relaxation and companionship. Too often, we spend more time in the kitchen than we do at the table with each other.

Our family tries to work around the situation. We get everyone involved. Even kids help in the kitchen; some of us grill meat or fish outside (Grrrrr!), while others prepare the

Barbara's Fruit Salad

1   orange, peeled and sectioned
1   red apple, cored, peeled, and sectioned
1   green apple, cored, peeled, and sectioned
1   cup strawberries, cut into fourths
1   cup green seedless grapes, cut into fourths
1   cup red seedless grapes, cut into fourths
1   cup pineapple, peeled and chunked
1   tangerine, peeled and sectioned
1   peach, peeled and sectioned
1   cup mini marshmallows
1   cup Cool Whip Lite

In a bowl mix fruit, marshmallows, and Cool Whip together.

SERVINGS: 6 TO 8

I love to add cherries to this recipe if they're in season.

side dishes inside. This way the whole family is spending time together, whether we even know it or not. Our family usually sets up meals buffet style to save time. Each person prepares his or her own plate, thus creating a mood of togetherness around the buffet. That way, one person is not stuck doing all of the work in the kitchen.

One technique we use to make time in the kitchen go faster is to prepare a dish in one pot. You can do this with entrees or side dishes. Casseroles are an easy way to save clean-up time, but many families don't get very excited about eating them. Over the years, however, our family has gathered some good casserole recipes that are tasty and simple to make. And to liven up these casserole dinners, I've added a few side dishes that can be made in one pot. Even if you're not casserole fans, maybe our

Matthew teaching his mother how to "work the line" in New Jersey.

Barbecue Turkey Kielbasa

■ BY BARBARA MANDRELL

1   pound turkey kielbasa, sliced
½   cup barbecue sauce

Brown kielbasa in a skillet. While turning, add the barbecue sauce. Be careful not to burn the sauce. You can add sliced onions to the kielbasa if you wish. (Brown them to transparency with the kielbasa before adding the sauce.)
SERVINGS: 4

See Matt's recipe for barbecue sauce on page 81.

Chinese Pepper Steak

■ BY BARBARA MANDRELL

My mom has about twenty sets of chopsticks that she bought when she was in Korea in 1967. When she makes Chinese pepper steak, pulling out those chopsticks is more fun and adds a little more oomph to the meal. For an extra flourish, she sometimes completes the meal with individually wrapped Chinese fortune cookies. (Believe it or not, she bought two big plastic bags of them from a catalog!) She might even serve some hot tea. All of a sudden she's created a very special dinner that is really quite easy. Even if it's a meal just for our family, it was really no more trouble to bring out the chopsticks and fortune cookies. And who knows? . . . It just might be your lucky day!

3	1.31 oz. packages brown gravy mix
3	cups sliced steak
½	teaspoon crushed garlic
2	tablespoons soy sauce
2	yellow onions, slivered
1	green bell pepper, slivered
1	red bell pepper, slivered
1	yellow bell pepper, slivered
2	stalks celery, sliced diagonally
1	small can sliced water chestnuts, drained

Prepare gravy in a saucepan according to directions on package. In a large skillet, quickly brown beef. Add the remaining ingredients and cook until the onions, peppers, and celery are soft. Stir in gravy and serve over white rice.

SERVINGS: 4

dishes will change your family's mind, as they have ours.

◆

When Mom's around, no one can get away without eating. Even the wild animals around our house are not exempt. She has a special area in our yard in Nashville where, every day, she sets out food for the deer, raccoons, and opossums. (In Aspen, she has a fox that she feeds.) She's serious about making sure her furry friends are fed every day, so you'll always find in our refrigerator a Styrofoam take-out box

Nathan feeding his mother after church. He loves chopsticks.

Chicken and Dressing Casserole

■ BY LOUISE MANDRELL

4	pounds chicken
2	teaspoons salt
2	peeled onions
4	stalks celery, sliced
1	carrot, sliced
1	can cream of chicken soup
1	can cream of celery soup
¼	cup cooking sherry
12	ounces evaporated milk
8	ounces seasoned breadcrumbs
¼	cup melted butter
1	cup slivered almonds

Cook chicken in a large pot with the salt, onions, celery, and carrot. When done remove the meat from the bone; tear chicken into small pieces. Purée vegetables in a food processor along with one cup of the basting. In a saucepan heat soups, sherry, and evaporated milk. Mix with vegetable purée. In a bowl mix breadcrumbs and butter.

To build casserole, pour one cup of the soup mixture in the bottom of a large casserole dish, topping with one-half of the stuffing and then half of the chicken. Repeat and finish by topping with the nuts. Bake in a 325° oven for 30 to 40 minutes.

SERVINGS: 8

Hot Chicken Salad Casserole

■ BY IRLENE MANDRELL

1   *can cream of chicken soup*
³/₄   *cup mayonnaise*
1   *cup sliced celery, cooked*
1   *cup sliced carrots, cooked*
1   *tablespoon diced onion, cooked*
1   *teaspoon lemon juice*
1   *cup cooked white rice*
¹/₂   *teaspoon salt*
2   *cups shredded cooked chicken*
1   *cup corn flake crumbs*
¹/₂   *cup almonds*

In a large casserole dish mix all ingredients except for the corn flakes and almonds. Add the corn flakes and almonds to the top crust. Bake in a 375° oven for 25 minutes.

SERVINGS: 4

Scalloped Mushrooms

■ BY MATT DUDNEY

6   *slices white bread, trimmed*
1   *cup sliced shiitake mushrooms*
1   *cup sliced portabella*
      mushrooms
2   *tablespoons butter, cut into*
      pieces
¹/₂   *pound white Cheddar cheese,*
      thinly sliced
1¹/₂ *cups heavy cream*
2   *eggs*
¹/₂   *teaspoon paprika*
      Salt and freshly ground pepper

In a greased medium-size casserole dish, layer as follows: half of the bread, mushrooms, butter pieces, and cheese. Repeat once. In a bowl mix cream, eggs, paprika, salt, and pepper. Pour over casserole and bake in a 325° oven for 35 minutes.

SERVINGS: 8

that's labeled "Racoon and Opossum Food" with a big magic marker. Woe be unto the human who should tamper with this container before Mom has had a chance to feed her friends in the woods. Most of us aren't even sure what's in those daily containers. (We're curious about the content, but not daring enough to risk being caught with our hands in the cookie jar, so to speak.) Judging from the robust look of the wild critters around our home though, it's safe to say they're eating quite well.

◆

When it comes to enjoying really simple foods, my grandfather Irby may have us all beat. His favorite dish cooked by my grandmother is "Maters, Taters, and Beans." When I first heard my grandfather say this, I had to ask him to repeat it.

"Maters, taters and beans," Irby repeated.

"Do you mean tomatoes, potatoes, and beans?" I asked.

Irby nodded with a smile.

I still could not picture an actual recipe, so I asked for

an explanation. Irby looked at me as if I were a loon.

"Matt, you eat here two or three times a month," Irby said incredulously, "and

Barbara filling one of the many bird feeders in her yard on a rare snowy morning in Nashville.

65

Scalloped Corn

■ BY MARY MANDRELL

1	10 oz. can cream-style corn
1	10 oz. can whole kernel corn, undrained
¼	cup chopped onion
¼	cup chopped green bell pepper
¾	teaspoon salt
1	egg
1	standard box corn bread mix
2	tablespoons melted butter
8	ounces sour cream
1	cup shredded Cheddar cheese

In a bowl mix the corn, onion, green pepper, salt, egg, and corn bread mix, adding melted butter at the end. Pour into a large casserole dish and bake in a 350° oven for 45 minutes. Remove from oven and top with sour cream and Cheddar cheese. Bake for an additional 15 minutes. Allow to cool ten minutes and serve.

SERVINGS: 4

Pinto Beans

■ BY BARBARA MANDRELL

Wouldn't it be nice if every meal were simple to prepare and took little time to cook? Seldom do these two traits go hand in hand, however. The easily prepared meals sometimes take longer to cook, or the quickly cooked meals require more preparation. An example of the first type of meal is one of my family's favorites: pinto beans with corn bread. This meal is easy to make, but the beans take time to soak and cook.

1	pound pinto beans*
1	ham bone or hog jowl
1	yellow onion, quartered
	Salt and pepper

Check beans for stones then soak overnight. After soaking, drain beans and place in large pot along with ham bone and onion. Fill with water to twice the level of the contents and cook until tender. Salt and pepper to taste. For variation, you can add one-fourth cup of chopped jalapeños toward the end of cooking.

When I make my mother's pinto beans, I like to add a tablespoon of sugar.

*This recipe also works for white beans.

SERVINGS: 6

you don't know what I'm talking about?"

Maters, I learned, are nothing more than sliced tomatoes. My grandmother peels off the skin and cuts the tomatoes in thick slices. *Taters* are home fries cooked with onions, and *beans* are just beans.

———◆———

A meal that Dad makes that many also find a bit odd at first is peanut butter pancakes. He tops his pancakes with peanut butter instead of butter. Wherever Dad acquired this twist (our theory is that it's a northwestern thing), his pancakes are out of this

Barbara and Mary cooking a meal together, 1981.

Chicken Chow Mein

■ BY IRLENE MANDRELL

4	stalks celery, sliced
1	medium onion, chopped
¾	cup chopped green bell pepper
3	tablespoons oil
2	tablespoons soy sauce
1	cup water
1	chicken bouillon cube
2	tablespoons cornstarch
1	tablespoon sugar
2	cups cooked and chopped chicken
1	10 oz. can bean sprouts, drained
1	6½ oz. can water chestnuts, drained
	Chow mein noodles

In a saucepan cook celery, onion, and green pepper in oil. Add soy sauce. Remove from heat. Mix water, bouillon cube, cornstarch, and sugar. Add to saucepan. Return to heat. After bouillon cube is dissolved and mixture is thickened, add chicken, sprouts, and water chestnuts. Heat thoroughly and serve over chow mein noodles.

SERVINGS: 4

Ratatouille

■ BY MATT DUDNEY

1   *medium eggplant, peeled and diced*
2   *yellow squash, diced*
2   *zucchini, diced*
1   *onion, diced*
2   *tablespoons butter*
½   *cup chicken stock*
1   *10 oz. can tomato paste*
1   *teaspoon garlic powder*
    Salt and white pepper to taste

In a large skillet sauté vegetables in butter until slightly soft. Add chicken stock and reduce liquid. Mix in tomato paste and dry spices while heating. Place mixture in a casserole dish and bake in a 350° oven for 25 minutes.

SERVINGS: 6

Turkey Pot Pie

■ BY MARY MANDRELL

1   *10 oz. package frozen peas*
1   *10 oz. package frozen carrot slices*
⅓   *cup butter*
⅓   *cup all-purpose flour*
½   *teaspoon salt*
¼   *teaspoon pepper*
½   *cup chopped onion*
¼   *cup chopped celery*
1¾   *cups chicken broth*
⅔   *cup milk*
2½   *cups cooked turkey*
2   *pie crusts (see recipe page 44)*

Rinse peas and carrots in cold water to separate; drain well. In a saucepan melt butter over low heat, adding flour, salt, pepper, onion, and celery. Cook until bubbly, add broth and milk, and bring to a boil while stirring. Boil for one minute, add vegetables and turkey, then bring back to a boil. Be sure to keep stirring. Place crust dough in a 9 x 9 x 2-inch pie pan and fill with mixture. Top with second crust. Bake in a 400° oven for 40 to 45 minutes.

SERVINGS: 6

world. The peanut butter melts just like butter, and if you like peanut butter, you'll love
these pancakes. He usually makes them for
us once or twice when we're in Aspen, but
we beg for them at other times as well.
They're so incredible that it's a wonder we

don't gain a dozen pounds every ti
eat them. (Come to think of it, we might!)

———◆———

Since it's just a short hop across the grid-
dle from pancakes to waffles, the pancakes
remind me of a waffle story involving Mom,

Corned Beef–Style Cabbage

■ BY MATT DUDNEY

1	*head cabbage, quartered*
2	*tablespoons pickling spices*
¼	*cup white vinegar*

In a large saucepan bring two
quarts of water to a boil. When
the water reaches a boil, add the
other ingredients. Bring back to a
boil and reduce heat to a strong
simmer. Cook until tender, then
drain and serve.

SERVINGS: 4

Try a little balsamic vinegar on the cabbage.

Chicken Soup

■ BY IRLENE MANDRELL

4	*pounds chicken*
8	*cups chicken broth*
2	*stalks celery, diced*
1	*large onion, diced*
3	*carrots, diced*
2	*cloves garlic, crushed*
1	*teaspoon pepper*

Boil chicken and section for soup. When done, strain broth for
soup. Combine eight cups of the broth with the stock and
bring to a boil. Add vegetables, chicken, and pepper. Reduce
heat and simmer for at least 15 minutes.

You can add cooked noodles, rice, or orzo to this soup for
a wonderful filler.

SERVINGS: 8

Potato Cheese Sauce

■ BY MATT DUDNEY

1	cup processed American cheese, softened
¼	cup finely diced tomato
2	teaspoons fresh basil, thinly sliced
2	strips cooked bacon, crumbled
¼	cup sour cream, softened
1	pint heavy cream*
1	pinch garlic powder
4	baked potatoes

In a double boiler, melt the cheese. When cheese is soft enough to stir, add the diced tomatoes. Heat until it stirs easily. Add the fresh basil and bacon, and heat for five more minutes, stirring often. In a bowl mix (with a mixer or a whisk) the sour cream and the heavy cream* until thin enough to go through a squeeze bottle. Add garlic powder and funnel into a squeeze bottle. Arrange potatoes on a plate and top with the hot cheese sauce. Using the squeeze bottle with the sour cream mixture, decorate the cheese in a sloppy but decorative way. Get creative.

SERVINGS: 4

*You may not need the whole pint of heavy cream to thin the sour cream.

Cheese Biscuits

■ BY MATT DUDNEY

2	cups all-purpose flour, sifted
1	teaspoon salt
1	tablespoon baking powder
½	cup shortening
½	cup milk
¼	cup melted butter
¼	cup warmed milk
6	ounces white Cheddar cheese, finely grated

In a bowl sift flour, salt, and baking powder together. Cut in shortening and mix well. Speaking of well, make a well in the mixture and pour in one-half cup of milk and work together until it can be stirred with a fork. Melt butter and one-fourth cup of milk in a saucepan and remove from heat. Roll dough to a one-fourth-inch thickness and cut into biscuits. Place on a greased cookie sheet. Brush with melted butter and milk mixture, then top with grated Cheddar cheese. For added flavor, sprinkle garlic salt on top. Bake in a 450° oven for 12 minutes and serve hot.

SERVINGS: 8

Louise, and Irlene. Mom tells it this way. "My sisters and I have always wanted to have a time, even a couple of days, where it was just we three girls—no husbands, no children, just we three sisters. Back in the late 1980s we were trying to carve out three days that cou be our time together. We were so excited about it, when all of a sudden, we were asked to cohost an awards show. We said yes, a little disappointed that our free-time

Buttermilk Biscuits

■ BY MATT DUDNEY

¾   cup butter, softened
3   cups all-purpose flour
4½   teaspoons baking powder
¾   teaspoon baking soda
¾   teaspoon salt
2   tablespoons sugar
1   egg
¾   cup buttermilk

In a bowl mix butter into dry ingredients. When fully combined, stir in the egg and buttermilk until the mixture forms a ball of dough. Roll and cut. I suggest a ¾-inch thickness with a 2½-inch diameter. Bake in a 400° oven for 15 minutes.

MAKES 16 TO 20 BISCUITS.

Chicken in Beer

■ BY IRLENE MANDRELL

4   boned and skinned chicken
       breast halves
4   cans cream of chicken soup
2   tablespoons soy sauce
1   cup beer
2   3 oz. jars sliced mushrooms
1   cup slivered almonds

Place chicken in a casserole dish. In a bowl mix all other ingredients. Pour mixture over the chicken and bake in a 350° oven for one hour, stirring occasionally.

SERVINGS: 4

had been taken. But it ended up that, unbeknownst to us, God had provided us those three days to sit and rewrite the script for the awards show. We spent those three days together—just us—writing. We'd still go to our respective homes in the evening, but during the day, all day, we'd sit around together writing and rewriting. We were really glad that we had that time set aside so we could write, but it didn't really count as our "just the girls" time.

"So fast forward ten years," Mom continues. "We've finally managed to pick another weekend for just the three of us to get together." (Wait a minute, wasn't there supposed to be something about waffles here somewhere?). "I'm getting to the waffles. My driver, Steve, drove me on my

Barbara and Irlene join Louise on stage at the end of her show in Myrtle Beach.

Corn Pudding

■ BY MATT DUDNEY

1	can whole kernel corn, drained
1	can creamed corn
2	eggs, beaten
½	teaspoon salt
1	pinch white pepper
2	tablespoons heavy cream

In a large casserole dish mix ingredients well and bake in a 350° oven for 25 to 30 minutes (or until firm).

SERVINGS: 6

bus to Atlanta on Friday evening around midnight and we picked up Irlene. She had just finished all of her work at a show she was doing there. We picked her up and drove to the Alabama Theater in Myrtle Beach, where Louise was performing that

night. We parked in the theater parking lot all day, and Louise came to see us on the bus a couple of times during the day.

"We enjoyed Louise's show that night. Then Louise joined us, and Steve drove us to a camping site in Georgia. We rented a car

Matt's Super Burger

2½	pounds ground beef
½	pound spicy breakfast sausage, patty style
1	tablespoon A-1 Steak Sauce
½	teaspoon garlic salt
1	egg

In a bowl mix ingredients well and form into 8-ounce patties. Grill well and serve as you would any hamburger. Expect compliments.

SERVINGS: 6

Tasty Home Fries

■ BY MATT DUDNEY

1	large potato, cut into wedges
	Olive oil
	Seasoning salt

In a bowl toss the potato wedges in olive oil while adding seasoning salt. Don't use too much. Bake in a 375° oven for 20 to 30 minutes depending on the thickness of the potatoes. Turn the potatoes twice during cook time.

SERVINGS: 1

Serve this with my cheese sauce. It makes a fun appetizer (see page 70).

After church each Sunday, the family goes out to eat lunch together. At the table we find Nathan, Matthew, Leigh Ann, Irby, Mary, and Barbara.

Wynelle's Southern Yellow Squash

■ BY BARBARA MANDRELL

2½ pounds yellow squash, sliced
1 tablespoon butter
Salt and pepper

In a saucepan boil squash. Drain off all of the water. Mash the squash as you would potatoes. (Some small chunks will not hurt anything.) Mix in the butter, and salt and pepper to taste. For a simple variation, double the amount of butter, slightly browning the squash in the pan.

SERVINGS: 4

and Steve checked into a nearby lodge, while we girls used the bus at the campsite as our get-away home base. There were hardly any other people there. For the next three days, it was just Louise, Irlene, and I in the bus. There was a gun club a few miles away and we went skeet shooting, trap shooting, clay pigeons shooting, and all kinds of shooting." (That's fine, Mom, but what about those cotton pickin' waffles?)

Simple Cheese Sauce for Vegetables

■ BY MATT DUDNEY

½   cup chicken stock
1   cup grated Cheddar cheese
     Heavy cream
1   teaspoon Cajun seasoning

In a saucepan bring stock to a boil and reduce to medium heat. Slowly add cheese to stock while stirring briskly. Add heavy cream to reach desired consistency. Add Cajun seasoning. Serve over freshly steamed vegetables.

SERVINGS: 6

Irlene, Louise, and Barbara enjoying a little "girl talk" with some chips and salsa on Barbara's bus, 1999.

"Ken's Favorite" Meatloaf

■ BY BARBARA MANDRELL

Ken loves, loves, loves meatloaf. He orders it, more often than not, when we're at home or at a home cooking–style restaurant. I never get tired of hearing him say, even after all these years, "nobody can make meatloaf as good as yours, Barbara." I've tried to pass along the recipe to Matthew, but the real truth is, it's never exactly the same twice. For an unusual twist, place three or four hard-boiled eggs in the center of the meatloaf before you bake it. It looks great when you slice it . . . and tastes good, too.

2	pounds ground beef
1	can tomato soup
1	1.31 oz. package Sloppy Joe mix
¼	cup chopped celery
¼	cup chopped bell pepper
¼	cup chopped yellow onion
½	teaspoon garlic salt
½	teaspoon pepper
1	egg
10	crushed saltine crackers
1	tablespoon honey

In a bowl mix all ingredients together, saving one-half of the tomato soup and the honey for a glaze on top. Mold into a loaf on a baking sheet, hence the name "meatloaf." Combine remaining tomato soup with the honey and pour over meatloaf. Bake in a 350° oven for 1 to 1½ hours.

SERVINGS: 4 TO 6

"Oh, yes," Mom says, "I did all the cooking and that's what brought this subject up. But, of course, Louise and Irlene helped with cleaning and everything. I have a toaster on the bus. One morning we decided to have frozen waffles. I saw Irlene put her waffles in there, and didn't think anything about it. But the next thing I knew, I turned around and Irlene's waffles looked so beautiful because she had sliced some bananas and put them between the waffles with some whipped cream. All of a sudden those frozen waffles became a magnificent thing. The whole weekend was just simple like that. All we did was cook, and eat, and shoot."

———◆———

And it's true, as Mom said earlier, home is wherever family is. Home cooking can be anywhere. For our family, home can be in Colorado, Tennessee, California, in a hotel, even on the road in our bus. The important thing is being together. And what better way to be together than by sharing a meal.

The 1948 Silverside bus.

CHAPTER 5

Pot Pies and Potholes
Recipes on the Road

By the time I was six years old, we had traveled more than 600,000 miles on Mom's tour bus. While this seems like a great distance, spending that much time on a bus makes it a new home away from home, and we learned to be comfortable. In the beginning, the conditions were a little like camping. Today, Mom's tour bus has luxuries that her first buses did not—things such as heat, air conditioning, and a reliable generator.

When you're forced to go without amenities you would normally take for granted, like heat and air, your true nature comes out. This is where the best stories (and recipes) come from. We learned our best recipes on the road through trial and error.

One mishap that comes to mind is the time Mom spilled a 2-gallon pot of chili down the bus corridor while we were traveling along an interstate at 65 miles per hour.

It took a long time to clean up. Rule No. 1: Don't spill a big pot of chili on the bus—especially if you're going up- or downhill.

Mom remembers our times on the bus: "For the most part, we didn't cook when Matt was aboard in his younger days. This allowed our adventurous child to discover many good places to eat while we were on the road. The food at the fairgrounds was always a particular favorite of his. But we also knew to ask the locals where the best small-town restaurants were."

Eventually, my mom learned to make some delicious "road" meals. And she has perfected these dishes to the point that she now cooks many of them at home. They're real road-tested recipes, you might say. Many are one-pot meals, which are the easiest (and most compact) to prepare, but they taste pretty darn good, too.

Rule No. 1: Don't spill a big pot of chili on the bus—especially if you're going up- or downhill.

*M*om began her career at the age of eleven, performing in Las Vegas two or three times a year and as a regular cast member of a television show in California called *Town Hall Party.* Home base was El Monte, California, and my grandparents drove her to these engagements in their car! After starting the Mandrell Family Band and relocating in Oceanside, California, Irby bought a Ford Econoline van, which had the name painted on the side and enough space inside to carry all the instruments and the

Pressure Cooker BBQ Chicken

■ BY BARBARA MANDRELL

I learned through experience about realistic menus for bus travel. I came up with some pressure cooker recipes that I still use at home. As you'll see, they are simple to make. But more importantly, there's only one pot to clean when you're done!

1	whole chicken, sectioned
1	cup barbecue sauce

Clean and skin chicken. Place a steamer tray in the bottom of a pressure cooker. Fill with about one-half inch of water. Toss the chicken in the barbecue sauce and place it in the pressure cooker, pouring the remaining barbecue sauce over the top of the chicken. Seal cooker. Cooking the chicken for 50 minutes, use high heat until the cooker starts to steam, then turn it down to low. The chicken will continue to cook for an additional ten minutes after it has been removed from the heat. Serve promptly. The meat will be falling off the bones.

SERVINGS: 4

band. Eventually, after moving to Nashville and starting a new recording career, they traveled greater distances to perform and required a different form of transportation than just a van or station wagon.

In 1970, when the 1948-built Silverside bus came into the Mandrell family's life, we regarded it as a luxurious blessing at first. Finally, there was room for all of our equipment . . . and us. But we couldn't afford a first-class bus, and the heat didn't always work, and the bus broke down regularly.

Barbara, age 12, performing in Las Vegas at the Showboat Hotel on New Year's Eve. She is backed by Red Foley's Band.

Barbecue Sauce

■ BY MATT DUDNEY

1	small onion, minced
2	tablespoons butter
1	garlic clove, minced
1	cup ketchup
¼	cup bourbon
3	tablespoons prepared spicy brown mustard
2	tablespoons Worcestershire sauce
1	teaspoon cayenne
1	teaspoon salt
1	teaspoon chili powder

In a saucepan sauté onions in butter until transparent, adding garlic toward the end. Add remaining ingredients and bring to a boil. Simmer for about ten minutes.

SERVINGS: 28

Mary and Irby on Barbara's first tour bus, the 1948 Silverside.

Money was tight, so we didn't always fix the problems.

Aunt Louise recalls that the "Old Bus," as she calls it, passed through many hands and logged many miles before it was parked at the Mandrell home. She says "parked," because that was its usual status, due to all of the mechanical failures. Painted gold with stainless steel trim, the old Silverside bus wasn't pretty, but it made the family feel as though we had achieved a new level of success. There was a kitchen and a lounge area in the front, a bunk room for the girls in the middle, and a small state-room for Mary and Irby in the back. They also had a bathroom, storage closets, and—the big luxury item—an intercom connecting the driver to the stateroom.

But even with these luxuries, there were long days on the road, and sometimes bad weather. Mom recalls a time when the family was traveling through a snowstorm to its next performance. The heater stopped working and it was so cold that a pot of water left in the kitchen sink turned to ice. The family tried to stay warm by huddling together to generate body heat. I was just a baby and I like to think they kept me in the middle of the huddle. Grandfather drove, knowing full well that, because they didn't have the most reliable bus, they could break down or get stuck any minute.

Ahead of them on the road that particular night, Grandfather spotted a truck driver whose truck had broken down. He pulled over and offered the man a ride. When the truck driver stepped on the bus, he thanked the family and said, "I was so cold outside and it is so warm in here." I guess he didn't notice that pot of frozen water in the kitchen sink!

Mom likes to tell that story as an example of times when people mistakenly think things are worse for them . . . because things can always be worse for someone else. In

the end the family traveled for twenty-four hours to the next job with no heat and nothing to eat, and Grandfather did all of the driving (as usual). But at least we weren't broken down on the side of the road.

As the band grew in popularity, so did the size of its paychecks and the quality of its transportation. The Mandrell Family Band became the Do-Rites, and grew to include not only Aunt Louise, Aunt Irlene, and Grandfather, but another guitarist as well. The band played small venues and fairs, so money was still very tight, and eating out was a treat when they had extra money. My mom and aunts remember the game they played to gather food for meals. During breaks at fairgrounds, Grandmother gave

Pork Tenderloin with Vegetables

■ BY BARBARA MANDRELL

3	packages pork gravy mix
1	pork tenderloin
4	carrots
2	onions, cut into quarters
12	red potatoes, cleaned or peeled
	Salt and pepper

Prepare the gravy mix according to the instructions on the package. Place all ingredients into the pressure cooker, starting with the meat and ending with the gravy. Seal and cook on high until the cooker starts to steam, then reduce to low for 50 to 60 minutes. Release the pressure and serve.

SERVINGS: 4

I use this same recipe with turkey breast and turkey gravy.

Barbara making peanut butter and jelly sandwiches on her tour bus.

each of her daughters some money and sent them out to get part of the supper. Each was to purchase a different dish: one was to find meat, one was to get vegetables, and one was asked to bring back dessert or drinks. The girls couldn't wait to get back to the bus to see what their sisters had bought.

Sometimes when they were on the road, however, the cupboards of the bus were bare and the family grew hungry. One time someone found a cookie and a fight broke out between Mom and Aunt Louise. They fought like animals over that cookie, but in the end, they split it. To this day, whenever Aunt Louise sees a cookie, she asks Mom if she wants to split it.

Mom recalls, "Sometimes we'd take a travel day off when we were touring

Potato Salad

■ BY MATT DUDNEY

3   pounds potatoes, boiled
3   stalks celery, chopped
1   teaspoon garlic salt
1   teaspoon salt
½   teaspoon white pepper
½   teaspoon onion powder
½   cup mayonnaise
1   tablespoon prepared spicy
       brown mustard

Peel and cube potatoes into a small bowl. Using hand, mix in remaining ingredients. You may need to use more or less mayonnaise. Chill and serve.

SERVINGS: 6

across the country. We'd be going down the road in a caravan of buses and I would decide to make us all a meal. When I finished cooking, our driver would radio the driver of the other buses that held our nine-piece band, the Do-Rites, and the crew.

"At the next rest stop, we'd pull in and all of us would have a meal at two or three picnic tables. The countertops, tables, and stove in our bus became the buffet. When the weather was good, the band and crew would play Frisbee or ball, or some would just work on a suntan. When you're away for a long time, it's a relief to get off the bus, visit with family and friends, and eat home cooking instead of restaurant food. At those times, the bus always seemed like home."

———◆———

Back in the days with the old Silverside bus, when Aunt Louise and Aunt Irlene were drummer and bass player with the Do-Rites, the band performed on a lot of "free stages"—stages apart from the grandstand, where the big-name stars performed. People were just passing by and could stop and watch the show. The bus had beds in it and bunks and

Miss Glenda's Chicken Soup

■ BY GLENDA DUKE

No one in our family really tours anymore, but my mom has kept the bus as a motor home. Over the years, our family has taken many vacations together on her buses. My dad particularly likes to use it for travel and quarters when he goes skeet shooting. When he plans a trip, Mom asks Miss Glenda, the caretaker of the Dudney household for over a decade, to make a pot of chicken soup for the road. Miss Glenda's chicken soup is tasty and easy to prepare.

6	*chicken breasts*
4	*stalks celery, chopped*
1	*yellow onion, chopped*
3	*carrots, chopped*
6	*chicken bouillon cubes*
2	*tablespoons instant chicken bouillon*
4	*cups egg noodles*
	Salt and pepper

In a saucepan boil chicken breasts, drain, and cool. Tear meat from the bones in bite-size pieces. In a large pot containing one gallon of water, add chicken, vegetables, and bouillon. Cook at a turning boil for 40 minutes. Add egg noodles and cook until tender. Salt and pepper to taste.
SERVINGS: 8

I really love Miss Glenda's soup.

Mary as the bass player for the Mandrell Family Band, 1965.

the stay, especially at fairs, we'd make discoveries, such as finding the folks who make the elephant ears and having them leave off all of the powdered sugar and stuff. We found that made a terrific bread for an evening meal.

"Or," Mom continues, "we'd find the vegetable gardening exhibition area and we'd buy these beautiful fresh tomatoes and fixings for salad. Or sometimes we'd buy fried chicken or local specialties."

For the most part in those days, my grandmother Mary was largely in charge of arranging for the meals (or cooking them herself) and for taking care of me while Grandfather, Mom, Aunt Louise, Aunt Irlene, and the rest of the band got ready for the show and performed. Sometimes she would even have to sew new costumes for the band between preparing (and even eating) our meals on the bus.

Though life on the road can be grueling, there are also many special memories. "All of the sweet, wonderful audiences make it all worthwhile," Mom reflects. And though most stops along the way don't allow enough time to really look around and explore the places you're visiting, the occasional chance to do some sightseeing at Carlsbad Caverns, or Williamsburg, or Niagara Falls makes for a nice break.

a complete bathroom with a shower. Mom remembers, "It was the only way we could afford to travel. We'd live in the bus there on the fairgrounds and at night we could hear the big shows in the grandstand.

"I remember lying in my bed and hearing all the big shows like Englebert Humperdink, or whoever, and thinking, 'I'm going to be over there someday.' But, meanwhile, we'd have to do four to six shows a day on the free stage for maybe a ten-day run. When you perform two hundred to as many as three hundred dates a year by doing fairs, rodeos, packaged shows in big coliseums, and clubs, you have to learn a lot of the survival techniques of the road. So, during the course of

I had many happy experiences on the road, including one state fair where I caught my first fish. But what do I remember most about being on the road during my younger years? . . . I learned to play cards.

It's no fish story and certainly no game of Go Fish. I learned to play poker at the age of five while on the road with my mom, grandparents, aunts, and the Do-Rites.

The band was opening for Tom T. Hall at a show in Georgia. President Jimmy Carter's mother, Miss Lillian, walked out to the bus in the rain to meet my grandmother. What a gracious lady. Meanwhile, Jimmy Carter's brother Billy came on board Tom T. Hall's bus to say hello. . . .

A friendly game of cards with some of the crew commenced as a way to kill some time before the show, and Billy Carter joined

Matt on tour with Barbara in Jefferson City, Missouri, 1974. (photo by Jim Miller)

in. After a while, Tom T. had to change into his stage clothes and get ready to do his part of the show. He gave his cards to little ol' me to finish out his hand. Since Tom T. also left his previous winnings in my care for

Fast Chicken Pot-Pie

■ BY MATT DUDNEY

2   cups chicken, cubed
    Oil
1   can crescent rolls (for 8)
1   can cream of mushroom soup

Sauté chicken in oil and set aside. Open can of crescent rolls and unroll dough. The dough is meant to break into triangles, but it should be separated into four rectangles instead. Place the four dough sections on a greased jelly roll tray. Place the chicken on the dough and spoon on the cream of mushroom soup (distribute equally). Fold the dough over and seal it together using water or egg wash. Bake according to directions on crescent roll can.
SERVINGS: 4

Matt and Barbara traveling on the tour bus.

betting, no doubt the adult, would-be card sharks smelled blood in the water and saw an easy path to taking a bite out of his winnings.

They kept raising the bets and I kept matching them. Finally, it was just Billy Carter and me, and Billy called on the last bet. What nobody realized was that Tom T. had already taught me a few things about playing poker, and I was pretty good at math. The pot was around fifty dollars. Billy had something like three 8s. Well, I had four 3s. Good enough. But it was still Tom T.'s money, so I received a dollar for my caretaking—which I still have—and good-sport Billy Carter signed it.

Of course, not all adventures were that pleasant. Mom would prefer to forget, but I

Grits with Cheese

■ BY MATT DUDNEY

½   cup grits
2   cups water
1   teaspoon salt
1   cup shredded Cheddar cheese
¼   cup melted butter
1   tablespoon Worcestershire
       sauce
     Cayenne pepper

Cook grits in water with salt according to directions on package. Stir in cheese, butter, and Worcestershire sauce. Add cayenne pepper to taste.

SERVINGS: 4

Matthew plays "Dueling Banjos" with his mother for fans who came to see her in concert at Abilene Christian University in 1989, while Matthew was a student there. (photo by Bobby Marshall)

relish recalling my encounter with a nine-foot alligator near the swimming pool at a Holiday Inn in Florida. Mom didn't believe me when I begged her to come see the alligator. (She was sure I was just being "The Boy Who Cried Alligator.") When Mom finally agreed to go see the alligator just to get me to be quiet, she warned me that I'd be in big trouble if I was just making it up. "Well, the alligator might not still be there, Mom," I declared, back-pedaling in an effort to prevent having my backside paddled. But sure enough, there was the alligator, and Mom couldn't get me and her away from there fast enough.

Not to give you the wrong idea about

my early childhood on the road, but one of my other favorite memories is being sort of used as bait by some of the band members. For example, we were by the pool at this motel one time, and the guys in the band were lying around in the sun when this pretty girl in a yellow bikini came up and sat on the side of the pool with her feet in the water. I didn't even bat an eye. I just got up from where I was, sat down next to her, put my feet in the water, and said, "Hi." I was maybe five or six years old. Then I said, "You know what my favorite color is?" She said, "What?" And I said, "Yellow." She was wearing that yellow bikini and just thought I

89

was so cute. That's why all of the guys would hang out with me—because they could meet all these pretty girls. Kind of like walking a puppy, I guess.

There were all kinds of fun times on the road, but generally it's a difficult life. As Mom says, "The only part of it that I really loved was the time on stage that I got to spend with my fans. Traveling on the road is what I had to do to get to do the ultimate great and joyful thing—performing for the people. I didn't really love all the miles, but your life is your life, and you make it as happy and as good as you can, every moment of it, and so we made it very comfortable and fun and enjoyable on the bus."

———◆———

As a traveling kid, I had lots of uncommon experiences. Some would say it was quite an unconventional childhood. But my mom always tried to give me the childhood that all my friends and peers had.

I remember several Halloweens during our time on the road. Mom would spend lots of time putting make-up on me and my brother and sister and dressing us in Halloween costumes. Then she would take us along with her during the preconcert activities and we would play "trick or treat" with the security guards, crew members, stage hands, drivers, musicians, and venue people. Amazingly, they always seemed to have candy ready to give us. (We found out later that Mom went around and supplied everybody with candy earlier in the day.)

Even Thanksgiving on the road was conventional. Although we couldn't always be home (for many years we worked the

Red Beans and Rice

■ BY MATT DUDNEY

1	pound dried red kidney beans
1	whole onion, chopped
2	cloves garlic, chopped
¼	cup chopped celery
½	pound peppered bacon, chopped
1	quart beef stock
1	teaspoon Tabasco sauce
1	teaspoon salt
1	whole bay leaf
¼	teaspoon ground thyme
3	cups cooked rice

Soak beans in water for at least four hours. Drain. In a large pot sauté onions, garlic, and celery with bacon. Add the beans, stock, and water until beans are covered (you will need to add water while cooking). Simmer. Add remaining spices when beans start to soften. Cook until tender and serve over cooked rice.

SERVINGS: 6

Thanksgiving show at Bally's in Las Vegas), Mom would always arrange for a traditional Thanksgiving meal. It wasn't the same as Mom's great cooking, but it was a special family time to give thanks for all we had together.

Many of my birthdays were also in Las Vegas, including my first birthday. Maybe that's why I turned out to be such a prodigious poker player. Mom always arranged for our time together, and we always had cake and presents.

But, of course, I wasn't the only kid on the road with the band. Even before Jaime and Nathan were on the road with the family, there were those other little kids, the Statler Brothers. Mom and her band opened for them for two-and-a-half years. The Statlers were great fun and brought out the little kid in everybody. They'd bring along all of these old cowboy movies. They'd have reels and reels of old movies starring Gene Autry, Roy Rogers, and the Durango Kid. I'd stay up with them eating popcorn and watching those over and over again. You can't do [t] that kind of childhood, on the road o[.]

———◆———

Today, our family has a half-million-dollar bus, designed and customized by my mom. She had a lot of help from two of her friends (both interior designers) in designing most of the bus. But when it came to the kitchen, Mom created it herself. She installed a microwave, refrigerator, Jenn-Air stove and grill, ice maker, self-cleaning oven, instant hot-water dispenser, and a double sink. She also bought the largest RV freezer on the market so we could take lots of food with us. It sounds like too many appliances to fit in just one vehicle, but Mom crammed it all into a compact space on her forty-five-foot bus. Today, we travel in much more comfort than ever before; but even long ago, it never mattered where we were, or what we were traveling in, home was where we were together.

Barbara putting Halloween makeup on Nathan.

Irlene's daughter Christina making cookies for her father, November, 1997.

CHAPTER 6

Cooking for Kids

If you can figure out what kids like to eat, it's a pleasure to cook for them. The foods they like best are no mystery—as long as they include sugar as a main ingredient. In this chapter, we've included recipes for cakes, cookies, brownies, and muffins—all the things that will make you a hit with the young ones.

We didn't stop there. The harder part is making other foods—and whole meals—that kids will eat. Fortunately, Aunt Louise is a specialist in this area. She not only makes food fun by transforming it into faces and animals, but she also invites kids to help her in the kitchen. It gives her a great deal of pleasure to see how involved kids become, and it gives her an opportunity to spend more time with them.

Our family has always had the tradition of having the younger ones help out. Mom and I enjoy time together in the kitchen even to this day. I love it when she calls me to ask about seasonings, baking temperatures, or ingredients. It's a way of sharing something today that started years ago when I was young and helping her in the kitchen. I get the same sense of pleasure when my brother Nathan helps me. It's a great way for us to spend time together.

Our family has always had the tradition of having the younger ones help out. Mom and I enjoy time together in the kitchen even to this day.

So, take a tip from our family: get your kids into the kitchen with you. They'll see how the meal comes together, and you'll have the pleasure of their company. It will be worth it even when they make a mess.

And they will make messes. I always say that, because of my clumsiness, I'm not especially fond of baking. But I still pursue it, because even though I have spilled more flour and eggs than anyone else I know, there's nothing more rewarding than a beautiful loaf of bread or a pan full of huge muffins. So I guess in some way, I am fond of baking. As long as there's that kind of result, I'll make it through the process. If you love to bake, then you're already a step ahead, and you will thoroughly enjoy these recipes.

When Aunt Irlene was four years old, my grandmother Mary was baking a birthday cake for my mom. One of the layers didn't turn out evenly, so when my grandmother iced and layered the cake, it turned out lopsided. Although Aunt Irlene was only a little girl, she tried to avoid hurting her mother's feelings by telling her, in her sweetest voice, "Mother, when it's my birthday, you don't have to bake me a cake. You can just buy it."

Mary made a fresh pie almost every day while her girls were growing up. It made her milkman very happy. He would let himself in through the back door and place what they had ordered in the refrigerator. She would always invite him to stay for a piece of pie. Sometimes he'd leave something extra in the refrigerator to show his appreciation.

My grandmother explained to us that the family made friends not only through their music, but also through their food. There's no better way to make good friends than through good things to eat.

Aunt Lynda's Brownies

Our family particularly likes this brownie recipe. It comes from our Aunt Lynda (Irby's sister-in-law). She comes to visit every year, bearing these brownies. We children would eagerly await her appearance and just to make sure would always ask Dad, "Is she bringing any brownies?" They really are that good, and they're actually more like cake than brownies. The icing is so rich that it takes a lot of effort to eat more than one.

This recipe is unusual because, in theory, mixing hot liquid into a dry mixture isn't supposed to work. Just mix the two together vigorously with a whisk, or use an electric mixer, and you'll be fine.

2	*cups sugar*
2	*cups all-purpose flour*
1	*cup butter*
1	*cup water*
1/4	*cup cocoa powder*
1/2	*cup buttermilk*
2	*eggs*
1	*teaspoon baking soda*
1	*teaspoon vanilla extract*

Grease and flour a jelly roll pan. In a mixing bowl combine sugar and flour. In a saucepan heat butter with water and cocoa until boiling. Pour hot mixture over flour mixture and beat well. Add buttermilk, eggs, soda, and vanilla. Beat until smooth. Pour into jelly roll pan and bake in a 400° oven for 20 minutes. Prepare the frosting five minutes before the cake is done and frost while hot.

SERVINGS: 12

When the Mandrell sisters were growing up, there were "special cookies" made just for Aunt Louise. She had a bit of a weight problem. And instead of making it hard on her by not allowing sweets, my grandmother bought sugar-free cookies and made an event of giving them to her.

One day Aunt Louise got very upset. She explained that my mom and Aunt Irlene were eating her cookies. Grandmother gave firm orders to the two sisters and they never again ate Aunt

Mary, Irby, Louise, and Barbara.

Aunt Lynda's Brownie Frosting

½   cup butter
6   tablespoons milk
¼   cup cocoa powder
1   pound confectioners' sugar, sifted
1   teaspoon vanilla extract

In same saucepan used for brownie mix, combine butter, milk, and cocoa. Cook four to five minutes until thick. Add the sugar and vanilla; beat well. Pour over hot brownies and top with nuts if desired.

SERVINGS: 12

Lemon Meringue Pie

■ BY MATT DUDNEY

1½ cups sugar
7 tablespoons cornstarch
1 pinch salt
1½ cups water
3 egg yolks, beaten
1 teaspoon lemon zest
½ cup freshly squeezed lemon juice
2 tablespoons butter
1 9-inch pie shell, cooked
Meringue

Combine sugar, cornstarch, and salt in a saucepan and stir in water. Bring to a boil over medium heat and cook while stirring for about five minutes. Remove from heat, cool slightly, and gradually mix in egg yolks. Return to heat and bring to a boil, cooking for one minute, stirring briskly. Remove from heat and slowly mix in lemon zest and lemon juice. Stir in butter. Allow mixture to cool to lukewarm and pour into pie shell. Prepare meringue and add to top. Bake in a preheated 350° oven for 12 to 15 minutes until meringue is golden brown. Cool before serving.

SERVINGS: 8

Meringue

3 egg whites
1 teaspoon freshly squeezed lemon juice
6 tablespoons sugar

In a bowl beat egg whites with lemon juice to soft peaks. Slowly beat in sugar until stiff peaks are formed.

SERVINGS: 8

Mary's Chocolate Chip Cake

1 package yellow cake mix
1 4-ounce chocolate pudding mix
½ cup oil
½ cup water
4 eggs
8 ounces sour cream
6 ounces semisweet chocolate chips

In a bowl combine all ingredients except for the chocolate chips. Blend well using an electric mixer. Flour the chocolate chips and fold into batter. Grease and flour a bundt pan and pour in the mixture. Bake in a 350° oven for 35 to 45 minutes. (Use the toothpick test.)

SERVINGS: 8

Louise's treats. It goes to show you that sugar-free or not, children will always want what they are not supposed to have.

Today, Aunt Louise has a food policy that keeps kids from overeating. It even stands when her daughter, Nicole, who's a super-talented teenager and straight-A student, invites friends over. She maintains that people can eat all they want on their plates, except for the last bite. Having grown up with a weight problem for a

Irlene's son Deric, second from right, and Barbara, were both born on Christmas Day, so after the Christmas presents are opened, the birthday cakes are brought out and the birthdays are celebrated.

Mary's Jiffy Banana Pudding

One of our family's favorite desserts is banana pudding, and my grandmother Mary makes the best we've ever eaten. This recipe is Southern in style (that is, very rich), but it's so good that you won't notice.

1½	cups cold milk
1	3-ounce box vanilla instant pudding
8	ounces Cool Whip
4	ounces sour cream
1	tablespoon vanilla extract
1	box vanilla wafer cookies
4	bananas, sliced

In a bowl beat milk and pudding until smooth. Add the Cool Whip, sour cream, and vanilla, and continue to beat until thoroughly mixed. Layer in a casserole dish as follows: vanilla wafers, banana slices, and pudding. Repeat, finishing with pudding on top. Sprinkle the top with vanilla wafer crumbs. Chill for 2½ hours and serve.

SERVINGS: 5

brief time, Aunt Louise is a strong believer in this policy. Modern mothers don't need to convince children that they must eat everything on their plates. "There's no need for a guilt trip," explains Aunt Louise. "Food is to be enjoyed, and kids should eat only when they're hungry."

Her daughter Nicole has a different interpretation: when she has friends over, she tells them they have to leave the last bite on their plates so everyone can see that they have left room for dessert. This is critical

One Mandrell family tradition is to give each child their very own birthday cake for their first birthday. They can eat it any way they choose. Here is Jaime on her first birthday.

Caramel Brownies

■ BY IRLENE MANDRELL

1	standard box German chocolate cake mix
1	can sweetened condensed milk
¾	cup melted butter
1	cup chopped walnuts
14	ounces caramels
1	cup semisweet chocolate chips

In a large bowl mix cake mix, one-third cup of the condensed milk, butter, and walnuts. Place one-half of the mixture in a greased 9 x 12-inch baking dish. Bake in a 350° oven for ten minutes. While cake is baking, melt caramels with the remaining condensed milk. After removing cake from oven, spread caramels over warm cake. Top with chocolate chips. Spread remaining cake mixture over the chocolate chips and bake for an additional 20 minutes. Cool and cut into 2-inch squares.

SERVINGS: 24

advice for most kids, judging by how much they love sweets.

Mom and Dad used a similar philosophy with us. We could take all of the food we wanted, but we had to eat it, unless someone else had prepared our plates for us.

◆

Whenever Aunt Irlene works with Aunt Louise at her music theater in Pigeon Forge, Aunt Irlene brings along her children, Deric, Vanessa, and Christina Louise. Aunt Irlene's children love to visit their Aunt Louise because she always makes special meals for them.

Irlene with her children: Vanessa, Christina, and Deric.

Peach Cobbler

■ BY MARY MANDRELL

½ cup melted butter
1 cup all-purpose flour
1½ cups sugar
1¼ teaspoons baking powder
1 teaspoon salt
⅔ cup milk
1 large can sliced peaches in syrup

Melt the butter in a deep pie dish or loaf pan. Mix the flour, one cup sugar, baking powder, salt, and milk, and pour into the pan. Layer the peaches on top and pour in the peach syrup, sprinkling the remaining sugar on top. Bake in a 375° oven for 40 to 45 minutes. Allow to cool for 20 to 30 minutes before serving.

SERVINGS: 6

One of these meals is a breakfast dish called "Eggs in a Frame." Aunt Louise cuts a circle in the center of a slice of bread, butters it, and heats it in a frying pan. She cracks an egg into the bread and cooks it slowly until it is set.

One night, after Aunt Irlene had cleared the dinner table, Christina came back into the kitchen, opened the refrigerator door, pointed inside, and demanded eggs! "She wouldn't stop saying 'Eggs!'" Aunt Irlene tells us, "until I had made Eggs in a Frame for her." By that time, Aunt Irlene was late to work. "Christina didn't even know what an egg was until she

Irlene's Chocolate Pudding Cake

1	egg, beaten
²⁄₃	cup sugar
¹⁄₂	cup milk
3	ounces unsweetened chocolate
1	cup sugar
¹⁄₂	cup shortening
1	teaspoon vanilla
2	eggs
2	cups all-purpose flour
¹⁄₂	teaspoon salt
1	teaspoon baking soda
1	cup milk
	Chocolate frosting

In a medium saucepan combine the egg, two-thirds cup sugar, one-half cup milk, and the chocolate. Stir constantly over medium heat until the chocolate melts and the mixture begins to boil. Remove from heat and cool. Cream the shortening, gradually adding one cup sugar (you will want your shortening to have a fluffy consistency). Add the vanilla and the last two eggs, one at a time, beating well after each egg. Sift the flour, soda, and salt together; add this to the creamed mixture slowly, alternating it with one cup milk, beating after each addition. Blend in the chocolate mixture last and bake in two greased and floured, 9-inch, round baking pans at 350° for 25 to 30 minutes. Cool and frost.

SERVINGS: 8

Homemade Chocolate Frosting

■ BY LOUISE MANDRELL

¹⁄₂	cup butter
³⁄₄	cup cocoa
3	cups confectioners' sugar
¹⁄₂	cup milk
1¹⁄₂	teaspoons vanilla extract
¹⁄₄	teaspoon almond extract

Beat butter in bowl while slowly adding the cocoa. Add sugar and milk alternately while beating. Last, add the vanilla and almond, beating until smooth.

SERVINGS: 8

started visiting Louise," Aunt Irlene grumbles.

That same night after work, Irlene and her children went back to Aunt Louise's house because Christina wanted even more eggs! Aunt Louise ended up making Eggs in a Frame for everyone, and they all stayed up late eating and watching movies.

◆

Whenever Aunt Louise used to come home from being on the road, Nicole would run to the door and say, "Mom's home. Let's party!" She knew that having her mom at home meant

Louise's daughter Nicole and Barbara's son Nathan, 1989.

Nicole's Banana Oat Bran Muffins

■ BY LOUISE MANDRELL

2   cups oat bran flakes
⅓   cup firmly packed brown
       sugar
2   teaspoons baking powder
½   teaspoon salt
1   teaspoon ground cinnamon
1¼   cups skim milk
2   tablespoons lemon juice
2   egg whites, slightly beaten
2   tablespoons vegetable oil
1   cup mashed bananas

In a large bowl mix oat bran flakes, sugar, baking powder, salt, and cinnamon. Next add milk, lemon juice, egg whites, oil, and bananas. Mix gently. Spray muffin pan with non-stick spray. Fill muffin cups almost to the top and bake in a 425° oven for 17 to 19 minutes.

SERVINGS: 12

Matthew kissing Jaime at their home in Hendersonville, Tennessee, 1976.

they'd do things a little differently—like wearing party hats during breakfast before school. Even when they were just having hamburgers for dinner, Aunt Louise would make a happy face on the plate: lettuce for the hair, pickles for the eyes, ketchup for a smile, and a piece of cheese for the nose.

Even the commonplace peanut butter and jelly sandwich has room for creativity, too. Aunt Louise butters the sandwiches on the outside and cooks them as though they were grilled cheese sandwiches. One time she made both grilled PB&J and grilled cheese sandwiches for a crowd of kids—the leftovers were all grilled cheese sandwiches.

When Aunt Louise has a party or a special event, she makes seating cards for the children. She bakes sugar cookies and puts each child's name on one with icing. They

Banana Bread

■ BY MATT DUDNEY

¾   cup butter
1½ cups sugar
1½ cups mashed bananas
2   eggs
1   teaspoon vanilla extract
2   cups all-purpose flour
1   teaspoon baking soda
¾   teaspoon salt
½   cup buttermilk*

Let the butter reach room temperature and mix well with sugar in a bowl. Add bananas, eggs, and vanilla. Sift together dry ingredients. Add alternately with buttermilk. Blend well (if you like nuts, add some now) and pour into a greased and floured loaf pan. Bake in a 325° oven for 1¼ hours.

SERVINGS: 10

*I like to use buttermilk powder that mixes with water. It can be found in the baking section of most grocery stores.

help the kids believe that the meal is just as much for them as it is for the grownups.

———◆———

When birthdays and other significant occasions come around, my mom brings out the "Special Occasion" plate. It is decorated with streamers and says "Celebrate!" around the rim and "It's Your Day" in the center. The plate came from a catalog years and years ago, and through the years it has become chipped. It's been in our family for a long time. But it still serves us well on special occasions. It's not

Matthew the "Birthday Boy" getting a birthday kiss from his mother.

Piña Colada Ice Cream

■ BY MATT DUDNEY

2	eggs
⅔	cup sugar
1¾	cups milk
2	cups heavy cream
2	teaspoons vanilla extract
¼	cup Malibu rum
½	cup pineapple purée

In a bowl beat eggs and sugar together until thick. Add remaining ingredients. Place in an ice cream churn and make as you would normal ice cream.

MAKES ABOUT ONE QUART.

This recipe contains alcohol ... it's for big kids only.

103

just for birthdays. Mom uses it as a traditional way to commemorate our family events. It can be for an award from school or some athletic event. It's just a simple way to focus on an accomplishment or an achievement and to let somebody know that he or she is special.

———◆———

Speaking of special occasions, Aunt Irlene's son, Deric, and my mom share a special occasion—they both were born on Christmas Day. "It is very special to me." Mom says. "Our birth times are only six minutes different. A friend once said to me, 'You know, Barbara, you were

Barbara reading a bedtime story to Matthew at their home in Hendersonville, Tennessee, 1972.

Banana Muffins

■ BY LOUISE MANDRELL

1	large egg
1	cup firmly packed brown sugar
4	mashed bananas
1/3	cup vegetable oil
1 1/2	teaspoons vanilla extract
1 1/2	cups all-purpose flour
1/2	cup oats
1	teaspoon ground cinnamon
2	teaspoons baking powder
1/2	teaspoon baking soda
1/2	teaspoon salt

In a bowl beat egg and sugar until fluffy, then add the bananas, oil, and vanilla. Mix remaining ingredients into batter until just moistened. Spoon batter into greased muffin cups and bake in a 375° oven for 20 minutes or until light brown. Cool and serve.

SERVINGS: ABOUT 16 TO 20 MUFFINS.

born so long ago that they probably didn't really keep track of birth times as precisely back then. Maybe Deric's birth was really *exactly* the same time as yours.' But really, it just means the world to me that Deric and I share that already-special day as our birthday. At family Christmas every year, he and I talk about it, and it just makes me very proud."

———◆———

Even an average school day can be made special when Mom is home and able to make school lunches. "Nathan likes to take his lunch to school. I take great pleasure in the fact that I'm usually the one that makes that lunch.

"Though I was on the road more with Matt and Jaime, I enjoyed making their lunches, too, whenever I could. I have this huge box with all of these different kinds of stickers. I would write a note with lots of fun stickers and put it in with their lunches to make it interesting and fun. One time when Jaime was in high school, just a few years ago, and she had been buying her lunch in the cafeteria, she asked me to make her lunch. When she opened her sack lunch and found the note inside, one of her girlfriends said, 'Oh, Jaime, your mom made you that lunch, didn't she? I remember when we were in grade school and your mom used to make your lunches and put those notes with the cute stickers in them for you all the time.' It's just a little thing, but I like that it wasn't unnoticed."

———◆———

Something on a larger scale, which is sure to get noticed, is a party that Mom has hosted and that might have some fun possibilities for you.

"In our home we have a soda fountain room, so that's probably what gave me this idea," Mom says. "One year I did a 50s party for my band, the Do-Rites. It was so much

Ann's Blueberry Muffins

■ BY ANN McCLUSKEY

2 *eggs*
¼ *cup margarine, softened*
¾ *cup milk*
½ *cup sugar*
2 *cups all-purpose flour*
3 *teaspoons baking powder*
½ *teaspoon salt*
1½ *cups blueberries*

In a bowl blend eggs, margarine, milk, and sugar until smooth. Mix in flour, baking powder, salt, and blueberries. Fill greased muffin pans two-thirds full and bake in a 400° oven for 25 minutes.

MAKES 12 TO 18 MUFFINS.

fun that we later put one on for Nathan and some of his friends. They thought it was a hoot, and totally enjoyed it. I'm sure their parents enjoyed helping them dress that way. The kids thought it was both fun and silly (and of course it's fun to be silly!) to slick that hair back and put that ponytail in or try to find something like a poodle skirt."

And she's right. There's no reason in the world that, just because kids today didn't experience 50s stuff firsthand, they can't have a ball in the same way their parents do when they relive the 50s.

And, of course, you don't have to have a

soda fountain for a 50s party. The magic of it is created by insisting that everybody come with their hair and their wardrobe in 50s style. You can even have a little contest in which the best dressed boy and girl (or couple, if the kids are old enough) win a prize. The prize doesn't have to be an expensive prize, just something that lets them know they were the best.

It's super easy to do this kind of party because you can have it for no reason at all, and it really doesn't have to cost much. You just make hamburgers or cheeseburgers, and you get french fries, or you might make

Aunt Louise's Meatloaf Mice

For Halloween one year, Louise created mini-meatloaves that were decorated as mice and served on a bed of marinara sauce. She called it "Meat Loaf Mice in Pools of Blood." If you try it on your kids, you may like it so much that you'll make it for an adult Halloween party.

2	pounds ground beef
1	tablespoon onion powder
3	tablespoons flaked parsley
1	teaspoon garlic powder
1¼	teaspoons chili powder
1¼	teaspoons salt
1	teaspoon black pepper
½	teaspoon ground sage
⅔	cup seasoned breadcrumbs
2	eggs, beaten
½	cup tomato sauce (or ketchup)
2	tablespoons Worcestershire sauce

In a large bowl combine meat and dry spices first, then add remaining ingredients. Form into eight mini-loaves or "mice." Bake in a 350° oven for 50 to 60 minutes.

SERVINGS: 8

Decorate the "mice" with spaghetti whiskers and tails, and olives for eyes.

it very elaborate and have onion rings, cherry Cokes, and, by all means, milkshakes.

Mom describes her old-fashioned method for making milkshakes: "Everybody else has these wonderful milkshake blenders and I have them, too, in the soda fountain room, but when I make milkshakes, as I often do for Nathan, I use a fork or spoon. I just get it on out and throw it in a glass. It's so thick you could stand a straw up in it, but I stir it all by hand. I just use vanilla ice cream and milk, and if you want a chocolate one, chocolate syrup. Put whipped cream

Barbara took Jaime and Matthew to see *Sesame Street* in Nashville, Tennessee, 1981.

Veggies and Rice

■ BY LOUISE MANDRELL

1	bunch broccoli, sectioned
1	cauliflower, sectioned
8	carrots, sliced
½	head red cabbage, sliced into strips
1	large onion, chopped
3	yellow squash, sectioned
14	ounces cooked brown rice
2½	cups shredded Cheddar cheese
¼	cup melted butter
2	tablespoons lemon juice
1	teaspoon Italian seasoning
	Salt and pepper

Steam veggies to desired tenderness. In a large casserole dish, layer the rice first, then the veggies and cheese. Mix the butter with the lemon juice and the Italian seasoning. Pour over mixture and bake in a 350° oven until cheese melts. Salt and pepper to taste.

SERVINGS: 8

Nathan eating his favorite meal, Kid's Delight, from the "Celebration Plate" to celebrate winning his ice hockey tournament.

and a cherry on top if you like."

Combine the fun wardrobe and good food with that great 50s music that everybody loves and you've got a fantastic party for kids and adults. Young and old games are always a fun addition, like Twister, for example.

Even without the 50s theme, you can have a great party with simple foods. When entertaining, it's important to make the meal—even the preparation for it—fun and memorable. For example, letting kids (or adults) make their own pizza is always a hit.

Kid's Delight

■ BY BARBARA MANDRELL

Every year, Jaime, Nathan, and I ask Mom to make the same thing for our birthday dinners. It's a simple hamburger dish but we love it. Perhaps it's the family tradition that we love best.

2	**pounds ground beef**
2	**tablespoons Worcestershire sauce**
1	**tablespoon soy sauce**
½	**teaspoon ground ginger**
1	**16-ounce can baked beans, drained**
1	**slice American cheese**

Make four hamburger patties, mixing in Worcestershire sauce, soy sauce, and ginger. In a skillet sauté burgers on stovetop until done. Drain grease and place beans on top of burgers. Cover skillet with a lid or foil and cook for an additional five minutes. Slice the cheese into eight strips and place on top of the burgers, making a criss-cross. Allow to melt, and serve.

SERVINGS: 4

This dish goes great with potatoes. See Matt's recipe for Home Fries on Page 73.

My parents have thrown very successful birthday parties for each of us by using the setting of a lake or a swimming pool. This makes instant fun for the kids. Even with the easy meal of hot dogs or hamburgers and all the trimmings, letting the kids put together their own burgers makes it more fun than just handing the food to them. They get to participate and create—as well as make their meal exactly the way they want it.

Nathan wearing his "chef's hat" and concentrating on his cooking style. He makes his mentor Matthew very proud.

———◆———

Like his big brother, Nathan loves to cook. When he first started cooking, Nathan knew that he, like all great chefs, needed a chef's hat. So he rummaged around the house and found this really cheap-looking Styrofoam hat. (Actually, it was more than cheap *looking*. It *was* cheap.) It was one of those hats that barbershop quartets use or that you see at political conventions, and my brother adopted it as his official chef's hat.

Well, seeing that there was much room for improvement in Nathan's hat, Mom didn't just stand idly by while her son cheffed around the house in an inferior hat. She rummaged around and retrieved a quality version of the same kind of hat that she had left over from her "Stepping Out" show a few years ago. Hers had a silk band, was made from the finest, most expensive material, and was crafted in Italy, like the straw hat Fred Astaire wore when he danced the soft shoe. It was the real deal. Nathan immediately recognized the superior quality of the new hat, which is now his official chef's hat. And with me, his big brother, giving him professional pointers in the kitchen (even basic instruction, such as turning his fingers under when using a knife on a cutting board), Nathan is well on his way to being skilled in the kitchen. At the very least, he'll be able to put on a good show.

Barbara and Ken having a dinner party for their friends, including Minnie Pearl, her husband Henry Cannon, and Eunice and Sargent Shriver, 1989.

Everyday Entertaining

Our family defines *entertaining* as cooking for people you love. If you think of cooking as an act of love, then it's a joyous event, and the preparation seems less stressful and more satisfying. Cooking with love is a practical philosophy and can help you put things into focus when those stressful moments occur, such as when the pie filling overflows into the stove, or when the sauce comes out too salty.

Aunt Louise puts it this way, "As an entertainer, I often find myself doing as much entertaining off stage in my home as I do on stage. And, of course, that means cooking—sometimes lots of it. For larger dinner parties, I always have Matt cater them, because he's my favorite chef.

"But when it comes to smaller gatherings," Aunt Louise continues, "I do the cooking. I've found that my attitude about meal preparation has changed over the years.

Some people grow up loving to cook, but I only cooked because it was a necessity. Finally, about ten years ago, I discovered that by taking a little extra time to discover what makes someone else happy, you can find happiness yourself by doing that certain something for each guest."

Aunt Louise adds, "I now make a point to remember what people like to eat, so that when they come back the next time, I can really please them. So now, cooking has become fun, something more than just turning out another meal."

So try to tune out the performance anxiety and the work and tune into how much you'll enjoy pleasing your guests. It's worked for my family for years. We hope that all of your parties are a success, and that you enjoy yourself as much as your guests enjoy your parties.

> **"Some people grow up loving to cook, but I only cooked because it was a necessity."**

*F*ood should always taste good, but presentation can make the experience of the food even better. People love to eat, and if the food looks beautiful, it makes the food taste that much better. Every dinner party does not have to include Crowned Rack of Lamb with Bananas Foster for dessert, but you do need to make the food look appeal-ing. The little extra things that you do will make your guests excited about eating what you have prepared.

I'm not saying this to worry you. If you are preparing food for a dinner party, my immediate advice is to relax and give yourself extra time just in case something goes wrong. Most often the work will go smoothly and the

Crab and Shrimp Puffs

■ BY MATT DUDNEY

13 ounces crab meat or shrimp, cooked
1   cup finely chopped celery
½   cup mayonnaise
3   tablespoons minced onion
2   tablespoons chopped sweet pickle
1   pinch salt and white pepper
50 puff pastry shells, cooked

Clean the crab meat well, removing all shell pieces. Drain and squeeze the crab meat. Combine all ingredients (except the pastry shells). Cut the tops off the pastry shells and discard. Stuff with crab meat.

SERVINGS: 25

Puff Shells

■ BY MATT DUDNEY

½   cup water
¼   teaspoon salt
¼   cup butter
½   cup all-purpose flour
2   eggs, beaten

In a saucepan boil the water and mix in the salt and butter. While stirring, mix in the flour (all at once). Be sure to stir well. Stir until a dough is formed and remove from heat. Add eggs and continue to beat until the dough becomes firm. Grease and flour a jelly roll tray. Place dough on the tray in teaspoonfuls. Bake for ten minutes in a 450° oven; reduce the heat to 350° and bake an additional ten minutes.

SERVINGS: 50

extra time will give you a cushion and reduce your stress level.

I've worked in restaurants that cater large events. It no longer scares me to cook for the huge numbers who attend these functions. Most of the time, it's just as easy to cook for two hundred as it is to cook for twenty—you just have to employ different techniques.

I always include appetizers when I'm making a "served" meal. They can be as simple as a cheese and cracker tray served with fresh fruit, or as complex as the first two courses of a six-course meal.

Birthday parties are fun for all ages.

Crudité Dip

■ BY IRLENE MANDRELL

½ cup sour cream
1 cup mayonnaise
1 package Italian salad dressing mix (dry)
4 teaspoons apple cider vinegar
3 tablespoons salad oil
Dill weed (optional)

In a bowl mix ingredients and sprinkle with dill weed (if desired). Chill and serve with assorted vegetables.

SERVINGS: 6

Avocado Soup

■ BY MATT DUDNEY

If you plan several courses for a sit-down dinner party, you may want to serve a salad or soup to follow your appetizer. (For a more casual party, serve soup.) If not, you can always just begin with the second course. The soup recipes I've included in this chapter are sure to impress your guests, and they take very little time to prepare.

1	avocado, peeled and chopped
1	cup chicken stock
½	cup milk
½	cup heavy cream
1	teaspoon lime juice
1	dash white pepper
1	dash salt
1	dash cayenne
	Sour cream
	Chopped chives

Purée avocado in a food processor, adding all ingredients, except sour cream, until smooth. Chill and serve with a dollop of sour cream and garnish with chopped chives. This is a cold soup but very savory.

SERVINGS: 6

Creamy Wild Rice Mushroom Soup

■ BY IRLENE MANDRELL

½	cup wild rice, uncooked
1½	cups water
2	green onions, sliced
½	pound sliced mushrooms
3	tablespoons butter
¼	cup all-purpose flour
4	cups chicken broth
1	cup heavy cream
2	tablespoons sherry

Wash wild rice in three changes of hot water. In a saucepan combine washed rice and water; heat to boiling point. Cover and reduce heat to a simmer. Simmer for 35 to 45 minutes until water is absorbed. In a large saucepan sauté onions and mushrooms in butter until onions are transparent. Add flour and stir, cooking for five minutes. Stir in chicken broth and bring to a boil. When thickened, add wild rice, cream, and sherry. Serve when the soup comes back to serving temperature.

SERVINGS: 4

Make a smaller size of a main dish you've cooked many times before, and serve it as an appetizer. That's a sure way to reduce your stress level and make you more comfortable.

We all have our own comfort levels about entertaining. Mom has *this* rule of thumb: "Beyond ten people, I have it catered—not because I'm lazy, honest. It's because I like to enjoy my guests and I don't get to when I'm the one that's working, busy as a beaver. I'm trying to make it right for everybody else, but when there's a caterer, I feel like I'm attending a party as one of the guests because I get to visit and be with everybody."

———◆———

Mom has always been a natural entertainer. Even her first real celebration after she and my dad were married was a bang-up success. Dad was still in the Navy. . . .

"When an officer gains rank, the other officers have what they call a wetting-down party, where they get together and drink and celebrate. On this particular occasion they were celebrating Ken's promotion from ensign to lt. j.g. Ken was the first, and to my knowledge the only, ensign to be assigned to the A-3, a tanker plane that was used for mid-air refueling and the largest jet the Navy landed aboard aircraft carriers at the time.

"All of the officers flying A-3s were much higher in rank than Ken—lieutenant commanders and commanders—so they and their wives were more like my parents' ages. But I thought it would be fun to have

Crab Rangoon

■ BY MATT DUDNEY

⅓   cup imitation crab meat
8   ounces cream cheese
1   pinch garlic powder
1   package large wonton wrappers
1   egg, beaten
    Oil for frying

Using your hands, shred the crab meat into a bowl. Mix with cream cheese and garlic powder. Shape into three-fourths-inch balls and chill well.

Place chilled mixture in the center of each wonton wrapper and seal wonton by bringing the center of each outer edge together. This will make the corners fold into each other. (Egg wash works best for sealing the dough.) Deep-fry in 350° oil until golden brown and serve with sweet and sour sauce.

SERVINGS: 6

Gazpacho

■ BY MATT DUDNEY

1 cup water
1 pound canned peeled tomatoes,
    drained
2 tablespoons sliced carrot
2 tablespoons sliced cucumber,
    seeded
1 tablespoon onion powder
2 tablespoons diced garlic
1/8 teaspoon cayenne
    Salt and white pepper to taste
2 tablespoons olive oil
2 tablespoons rice wine vinegar

In a food processor purée all ingredients except the oil and vinegar. When smooth, stir in oil and vinegar. Serve chilled.

SERVINGS: 4

Shrimp Dip

■ BY IRLENE MANDRELL

12 ounces cream cheese, softened
1 teaspoon horseradish
1/4 teaspoon garlic powder
1 dash salt
1/2 cup mayonnaise
1/2 teaspoon Worcestershire sauce
    Milk*
1 6-oz. can shrimp, drained

In a bowl mix all ingredients except milk and shrimp. Next, add the milk slowly, mixing until desired consistency is reached (the amount of milk needed may vary*). Gently stir in shrimp by hand (do not use a mixer). Serve with crackers or potato chips.

SERVINGS: 6

a wetting-down party just for us wives to celebrate Ken's promotion. I remember it was around Halloween because I bought these little plastic bugs, spiders, and worms to put in the drinks as a joke. That was about the extent of the decorations. And then I just had some things like chips and dips and maybe some nuts. I really had never given parties and didn't really know much about it.

"But I was determined to be the proper hostess for all of us girls. I designated myself as the bartender even though the only alcohol I'd ever had in my life was one blackberry wine mixed with 7-Up and maybe a taste of beer. I didn't know anything about different types of drinks, but here I was tending bar for the wives of my husband's fellow officers. I had my chips and

Mary holding her Mother's Day cake.

Leigh Ann's Spicy Vegetable Dip

8	ounces cream cheese, softened
3	tablespoons mayonnaise
1/3	cup chili sauce
1/3	cup minced onion
1/2	teaspoon Worcestershire sauce
1/4	teaspoon horseradish

In a bowl mix all ingredients well and top with paprika. Chill and serve with fresh raw vegetables.

SERVINGS: 6

Fried Oysters

■ BY MATT DUDNEY

½   pound oysters, cleaned
1   cup egg wash
1   cup breading mix
     Oil

Dip each oyster in egg wash
(made by beating 3 eggs with
one-half cup water) and cover
with breading mix. Deep fry in
350° oil until golden brown.

SERVINGS: 4

Black Bean Salsa

■ BY MATT DUDNEY

4   large tomatoes, peeled and
     chopped
1   large onion, chopped
2   tablespoons chopped cilantro
3   tablespoons chopped fresh
     jalapeños
1   tablespoon rice wine vinegar
2   tablespoons lime juice
1   10 oz. can black beans
     Salt and white pepper

In a bowl mix by hand all ingredients (including bean juice),
adding salt and pepper to taste. Chill before serving, or heat and
serve with blackened fish. This can also be served under fried
oysters (as above).

SERVINGS: 6

dip and peanuts going and I was tending bar and somebody even brought the game Twister, which was all the rage at the time, and boy, I just thought to myself, 'This is a big-time party you're putting on.'

"Well, everybody ordered drinks by telling me what was in them and then I'd make it. If they wanted a screwdriver, I didn't know any better, so I'd make it with half a glass of vodka and half a glass of orange juice. It sounded good to me—fifty-fifty. I made all the drinks that way. I've got to tell you, we were only about an hour and a half into the party when all of the officers' wives were on the floor playing Twister. Yes sir, it was a good party. We had a real good wetting-down party. Those ladies didn't need pilots or bombardiers to know about flying high or getting bombed that night. All they needed was one naive bartender in charge of their refueling."

———◆———

Many years later, once Mom had become an experienced host and gladly left the bartending to others, she threw a party with a mariachi band for her friends. She decorated with some little red chili-pepper lights on a string and just had the caterer make a variety of wonderful Mexican dishes. For an added touch, she had two piñatas, one for the men and one for the women, filled not with candy but with little trinkets

Fajitas

■ BY MATT DUDNEY

2	pounds chicken or beef, sliced
	Olive oil
1	green bell pepper, sliced
1	red bell pepper, sliced
1	large onion, sliced
1	tablespoon blackening spices

To really do this correctly use an iron skillet. In a skillet, sauté the meat in olive oil. Add vegetables, finishing by topping with spices. Mix thoroughly and cook until crisp-tender. Serve with tortillas and fresh lettuce, tomatoes, guacamole, and shredded white Cheddar cheese.

SERVINGS: 4

See my recipe for blackening seasoning on page 136.

Roast Beef Tenderloin and Mashed Potatoes

■ BY MATT DUDNEY

If you like the idea of dramatic presentation, consider a meat entrée that can be carved in front of your guests. For ideas, see my chapter on wild game (for duck or goose recipes). If you like the idea of serving beef, but not carving in front of an audience, try cooking a beef tenderloin and carving it in the kitchen.

1	*whole beef tenderloin*
¼	*cup minced garlic*
	Salt and freshly ground pepper
	Olive oil

Clean tenderloin of sinew and fat. Roll tenderloin in minced garlic, salt, and pepper. Sear in olive oil in a large skillet on stovetop. Place in a 350° oven on a jelly roll tray and bake until desired internal temperature is reached. This is normally served rare to medium rare. For rare the internal temperature will be 140°. Allow meat to rest for ten minutes before slicing into eight pieces. Serve with mashed potatoes (below).

SERVINGS: 8

Roasted Garlic Mashed Potatoes

■ BY MATT DUDNEY

2	*cloves garlic*
	Olive oil
3	*pounds potatoes, peeled and cubed*
½	*cup butter*
¼	*cup heavy cream*
	Salt and white pepper

To roast garlic, cut the top off of the garlic clove, rub with olive oil, place in a small oven-safe dish, and bake in a 400° oven until golden brown or the inner parts of the garlic are soft. Squeeze from the bottom to remove the garlic from the skin.

In a large pot boil potatoes until soft. Remove from heat and strain. Place back in pot, return to heat, and mash, mixing in butter and heavy cream. You may not want to add all of the butter or heavy cream; it's your choice. Add roasted garlic, mixing well, and salt and pepper to taste.

SERVINGS: 6

like key chains, pocket knives, bottle openers, fishing lures, etc. for the men and plastic bottles of nail polish, lipstick, eye pencils, etc. for the women. It was a wonderful party, and besides, how often do adults get to break open piñatas!

———◆———

Another interesting event at our house was a school fund-raiser with about fifty couples. We held the party around our indoor pool and the theme was "Western Night." Everybody dressed up as cowboys and cowgirls and we threw a few bales of hay around for decoration. A local restaurant donated a whole pig. Mom, Aunt Louise, and Aunt Irlene were the hosts for the party. More precisely, they were the official waitresses for the evening. Irlene had the additional responsibility of carving the pig. It really was a smashing success. The atmosphere was great and we raised a lot of money for the school.

Nashville hosts an event for country music fans each summer called Fan Fair. Here, Barbara, Ken, and Matthew attend Barbara's first breakfast for fan club members, 1973.

Cinnamon Chicken

■ BY MATT DUDNEY

2	frying chickens, quartered
1/3	cup lemon juice
4 1/2	tablespoons olive oil
3/4	teaspoon ground cinnamon
1	teaspoon dried oregano
3/4	teaspoon salt
3/4	teaspoon white pepper

Mix lemon juice, olive oil, and spices. Place chicken in mixture and marinate for at least one hour, turning often. Broil for 30 minutes, basting often. Turn chicken once while cooking.

SERVINGS: 6

Barbara's Breakfast Burrito

Brunch is a great alternative to a dinner party and has the potential to become a wonderful, leisurely party. Your menu choices are endless. Everyone likes breakfast foods, from omelets to Belgian waffles with fresh berries. But this recipe is sure to intrigue your guests and get the conversation started. I was working on a movie once, sitting in the makeup chair early one morning, when someone asked me what I wanted from the catering truck, a roll or a coffee or a breakfast burrito. I said, "A burrito for breakfast?" They brought me one, and I've been making them ever since.

2	slices fried bacon
2	scrambled eggs
	Shredded cheese
1	flour tortilla
	Salsa

On a plate, roll bacon, eggs, and cheese into a tortilla. Fold up one-fourth of the bottom of the tortilla, then fold in both sides. Finish rolling and serve with salsa. You can also scramble green onions, bell peppers, and cheese with your eggs before you make the burrito.

SERVINGS: 1

After the party, the manager of the restaurant that had been catering came over to Mom and said, "I know you've got better things to do, Barbara, but if you ever want a job as a waitress, you've got it." Mom was thrilled to hear that because, as she says, "I love serving people and I *am* fast. I said I would be glad to help anybody, but not where I have to do the bill and figure up the cost and make the change. I don't want to do that, but I'll serve, clean up, cook, whatever. I love it all."

———◆———

Of course, good entertaining can be a lot simpler. One time Mom came home from a hard day working an event and found Dad and our good friend Lynn Swann (the sports commentator and former All-Pro wide receiver for the Pittsburgh Steelers) visiting. Mom came in with a gift basket of fruit and Dom Perignon that she had received the day before.

Well, it was getting to be about supper-time and Mom was really too tired to do anything in the kitchen, but she really wanted the chance to visit with Lynn, so she asked him, "Do you mind if we just order in pizza and kind of take it easy?" Lynn said that sounded just fine to him. So they nibbled on the fruit and enjoyed delivery pizza and expensive champagne. Sometimes the best entertaining involves no production at all—just a relaxed, casual evening with good friends.

Matt's Favorite Omelet

3 eggs
2 tablespoons skim milk
3 mushrooms, sliced
¼ cup cooked Italian sausage, crumbled
3 tablespoons grated mozzarella cheese
3 tablespoons marinara sauce, heated

In a bowl beat eggs with milk and cook as you normally would for an omelet. Flip omelet. Stuff with mushrooms, sausage, and cheese. Fold and continue to cook. Serve topped with marinara sauce.

SERVINGS: 1

Barbara's Sparkling Fruit

1   orange, peeled and sectioned
1   green apple, peeled and sliced
1   red apple, peeled and sliced
1   cup strawberries, quartered
1   cup green seedless grapes,
       quartered
1   cup red seedless grapes, quartered
1   cup pineapple chunks
1   tangerine, peeled and sectioned
1   peach, cleaned and sliced
1   cantaloupe, peeled and chunked
1   honeydew melon, peeled and
       chunked
2   cups sparkling wine or grape juice

In a large glass bowl mix fruit and liquid together. Chill for at least one hour. Toss before serving.

SERVINGS: 4

———◆———

On the other end of the spectrum (which can be just as fun) was a party we threw right after Nashville finally got its NHL team, the Nashville Predators. Our whole family had been hoping Nashville would get an NHL franchise for years. We were so excited that we had a party for all of the players and staff and their families—about a hundred and eighty people.

In order to accommodate a crowd that size, we knew we had to keep it simple—we just needed to have a big cocktail party. The key, though, was going really heavy on the hors d'oeuvres. There was plenty of food for everybody to easily have the equivalent of a nice—and even a well-balanced and nutritious—meal simply by working their way

Nathan gives his Grandfather Irby a giant cookie for his birthday, October 1998.

Special Pumpkin Bread

■ BY MARY MANDRELL

3	cups sugar
1	cup cooking oil
½	teaspoon grated orange peel
3	eggs
1	large can pumpkin purée
½	teaspoon salt
½	teaspoon baking powder
1	tablespoon baking soda
3	cups all-purpose flour
1	tablespoon ground cloves
1	tablespoon ground cinnamon
1	tablespoon grated nutmeg
1	cup chopped nuts

In a large bowl mix sugar, oil, orange peel, and eggs, adding pumpkin at the end. Set aside. In another bowl mix by hand all other ingredients and add to liquid. Bake in two greased loaf pans for 70 minutes in a 350° oven.

SERVINGS: TWO LOAVES

My grandmother always uses walnuts in this recipe.

Barbara's Kabobs

Kabobs are a fun party food for less formal occasions. And you can custom build each kabob to the specific tastes of your guest.

6   ounces cubed beef
1   large onion, cut into wedges
1   large green bell pepper, cut
      into wedges
6   large mushrooms
1   6½-ounce can of pineapple
      chunks, drained
      Salt and pepper

Alternate ingredients on two skewers. Marinate in a shallow dish for at least one hour, turning twice. Grill or broil until meat is cooked to desired temperature.

SERVINGS: 2

See my mom's steak marinade on page 25.

Chicken and Shrimp Kabobs

■ BY MATT DUDNEY

4   ounces cubed chicken
2   ounces peeled shrimp
1   10 oz. can pineapple spears,
      cubed
¼   zucchini, sliced diagonally
¼   yellow squash, sliced diagonally
6   large mushrooms
¼   cup teriyaki sauce

Using two skewers, alternate ingredients. Roll in teriyaki sauce and grill or broil. Serve with steamed rice.

SERVINGS: 1

See my recipe for teriyaki sauce on page 160.

through the wide selection of hors d'oeu-vres. The plan must have worked because folks stayed well beyond the customary time for a basic cocktail party. That's always a good sign that your guests are having a good time and enjoying the food, which is pleasing to the guests as well as the hosts.

———◆———

So, if there's one word of advice we have about entertaining, it's simply to have fun. There can sometimes be a lot of planning and work, but approaching entertaining as an opportunity to do something nice for people you care about makes it a pleasure for everybody.

Sausage Milk Gravy

■ BY BARBARA MANDRELL

2 tablespoons sausage grease
1 patty sausage, cooked
½ cup all-purpose flour
   Milk
   Salt and pepper

Use the same pan for this recipe that you use to cook the breakfast sausage; it makes this stuff even better. Crumble the sausage into small pieces and add to hot grease. Sprinkle flour into grease, stirring constantly until all is combined. Add milk to desired consistency, adding salt and pepper to taste. (This gravy requires lots of salt and pepper, but keep tasting it as you add the seasonings to make sure you've perfected the taste.)

SERVINGS: 6

This gravy is great poured over biscuits, eggs, sausage, bacon, toast, or sliced bread. Heck, this stuff's so good I'd probably like it on cardboard.

Camping at Sheep Creek, Washington, 1986.

CHAPTER 8

Campfire Cooking

*M*y parents started taking us on camping trips when we were still quite small. Nathan and I in particular had always appreciated making forts, both inside and outside the house, but that was the extent of our training to "Be Prepared" for the outdoors. But the early contact with the outdoors has given us a deeper appreciation of nature. We've all found that being outside is wonderfully relaxing and allows us to enjoy our environment and look into ourselves. But as a child, I often quipped, "Most of the time, when I look into myself, I see an empty stomach."

Over the years we've built many of our family reunions around eating and camping. Every summer, in fact, Mom hosts an event called Kamp Kuzzins. She borrowed the idea from the Lunsford family of Olney, Texas. The idea is to bring together all the young cousins so they can spend time together in a camp-like atmosphere. Dad built a campsite in the woods about ten years ago and that's

> **W**e've all found that being outside is wonderfully relaxing and allows us to enjoy our environment and look into ourselves.

where Mom holds the event. "I just think it's important for these cousins, who otherwise might not have a chance to get together and have fun, to have some time together—much in the same way I feel it's vital that we have Mandrell Family Christmas every year. I take pictures at Kamp Kuzzins every year and I make each Kuzzin a little photo album. It's all part of what I hope will help them preserve memories of their time together and help them bond forever."

Mom has taken the concept of going to camp a bit further and taken the radical step of including actual camping in the activities for Kamp Kuzzins. The Kuzzins backpack into their campsite, set up tents, and build a fire for cooking. Mom is a dedicated camp director, and the kids always have a ball. (Many of the adult family members enjoy camping, but many of us aren't sure we have enough stamina to do what Mom does with Kamp Kuzzins every year.)

$\mathcal{M}$om uses a particularly inventive recipe during Kamp Kuzzins. It's always a hit. Best of all, it's simple to make and even easier to clean up. She takes a large, heavy, paper grocery bag and puts strips of bacon in the bottom. She rolls up the top of the bag and places it on a grill over a fire. (The fire is composed of nothing but coals, so the bag will not burst into flames.)

The bacon cooks in its own grease and, miraculously, the bag doesn't fall apart. She opens the bag, turns the bacon over, cracks an egg on top of the bacon after it's done, and reseals the bag. The bacon will continue to cook a little more, and conse-

Tuna Salad

■ BY MATT DUDNEY

I've always been a big fan of sandwich spreads for camping or traveling. They're convenient because you don't have to pack meat, cheese, or condiments—just bread and a container of sandwich filler. I make sure the food never spoils by packing it in small coolers when I travel or camp. I also use airtight containers so I can place the food on ice without it becoming waterlogged.

1	**can tuna, drained**
1	**stalk celery, chopped**
½	**teaspoon Old Bay seasoning**
2	**tablespoons mayonnaise**
1	**pinch garlic powder**
	Salt and pepper

The important thing here is to completely drain all water from the tuna. Mix all ingredients in a bowl. Add salt and pepper to taste.

SERVINGS: 4

Tuna Salad with Cheese

■ BY MATT DUDNEY

1	**can tuna, drained**
1	**stalk celery, chopped**
1	**pinch garlic powder**
2	**tablespoons mayonnaise**
1	**tablespoon Parmesan cheese**

Drain all water from the tuna. In a bowl mix all ingredients thoroughly. This is a great snack to eat with saltine crackers.

SERVINGS: 4

quently, the heat cooks the egg. When both are done, she removes the bag from the fire and tears it open. Now she has a meal in a brown paper bag, which also works as a serving plate. This technique sounds a little weird but it really works. My cousins go crazy over the notion of breakfast in a grocery bag.

◆

Even though Mom and the Kamp Kuzzins spend a couple of nights just a short hike from Fontanel, our home in Tennessee, the night noises in our valley can get pretty spooky. One year there were a couple of hoot owls hooting and a coyote howling in the distance. Curiosity even prompted one of our six cats, Vanderbilt (named in honor of the Nashville university's black and gold colors), to investigate the strange

Matthew came to visit the "Kamp Kuzzins" and to check out the campsite they had set up, 1998.

Chicken Salad

■ BY MATT DUDNEY

20 ounces chicken, cooked and shredded
2 stalks celery, chopped
½ teaspoon garlic powder
1 pinch Old Bay seasoning
1 pinch salt
1 pinch white pepper
1 pinch onion powder
¼ cup mayonnaise

In a bowl mix ingredients thoroughly using your hands. You may want to use more or less than one-fourth cup of mayonnaise. Chill and serve.

SERVINGS: 4

campers. Despite the fact that our formidable dogs Dandy and Chouette were among the campers already in the tent with everyone, Vanderbilt joined them in the tent, too. Togetherness is great! Crowded, but great!

———◆———

Whenever anyone in our family goes on a road trip, Mom packs food and drink. Her packages end up more like provisions for an extended hike into the wilderness. They always contain sandwiches, fresh fruit, and loads of chips and cookies. It's not really camping, but we'd certainly be prepared if the occasion came up.

But Mom hasn't always been such an experienced camper. She recounts her first

Pimiento Cheese

■ BY MARY MANDRELL

1	pound processed American cheese
¼	cup margarine
1	jar chopped pimientos
1	tablespoon sugar
1	tablespoon white vinegar
1	cup mayonnaise

Melt cheese and margarine in a bowl in the microwave. Add pimientos, sugar, vinegar, and mayonnaise. Mix well. (Add more mayonnaise if necessary.) Serve on bread or as a dip with crackers.

SERVINGS: 6

Crab Salad

■ BY MATT DUDNEY

16	ounces lump crab meat
3	tablespoons mayonnaise
1	pinch salt
1	pinch white pepper
½	teaspoon dried dill weed
½	teaspoon Old Bay seasoning
1	stalk celery, chopped

Clean crab meat of all shell pieces and squeeze dry. In a bowl mix all ingredients. Serve on bread or as a dip.

SERVINGS: 4

You can use imitation crab meat with this recipe and no one will be able to tell.

camping trip with my dad here. "We were newlyweds and we went camping at this lovely spot in Washington state. Because Ken was in the military, we could check out camping gear, so that was nice. I'd never been camping, but I decided I'd jump in with both feet and act like I knew what I was doing. So here I am. I'm a first-time camper. Our dinner that night was steak and home fried potatoes and some sort of vegetable out of a can. And I had made a salad that I had carefully covered. And are you ready for the dessert? It was strawberry shortcake. For camping! Ken said, 'Barbara, this tastes delicious and it's fabulous but you really don't have to do all this for camping. So I relaxed after that."

———◆———

My parents didn't get to go camping again until after Jaime and I were born. We all went with Dad's family to a place called Sheep Creek, which is where we held a family reunion with the Dudney family for many years. Grandma Johnson (Dad's grandmother) was the driving force behind this reunion, which we did every summer in July.

All we kids would get our own little tents. Mom recalls, "Matt always used to pick out an adventurous place for his tent. His favorite spot was on this little cliff right next

Matthew camping in Sheep Creek, Washington, with his Great Grandma Johnson, 1977.

to the creek shore. He liked it because he could hear the running water. It was a beautiful spot and there he'd be with his little tent and campfire and little supply of food."

On Sundays during the reunions, Grandma Johnson made sure that we would

Matthew teaching Nathan how to fish during a family camping trip in Sheep Creek, Washington.

perform our own worship service on Sunday mornings, and Grandma Johnson and Aunt Martha and some of the other aunts and Mom would go walking with some of the kids and pick a few of the many wildflowers in the area. They would fix an altar with these beautiful wildflowers. Mom would usually lead the singing.

On one of the Sundays, Mom was taking song requests, as was the custom, and

Nathan, who was just a toddler, raised his little hand up and said, "Silent Night." Well, they sang it and everyone had to agree that singing "Silent Night" in that beautiful forest on a summer Sunday morning in the month of July meant more to them than it ever had. Everyone really focused on the meaning of the song.

Another tradition at Sheep Creek was a rotating schedule of chores, such as cooking for the group or washing the dishes. Two of the families would be assigned a day to cook for everyone. It was a great way to get the individual families to work together while doing something for the larger family group. Even the little children were assigned tasks. Everybody pitched in and pulled together and it was fun. We knew ahead of time which responsibilities we'd have for which days and could plan ahead to bring the necessary

The only way to get a warm bath while camping in Washington state was to heat water over an open fire and bathe in a trash can. Nathan loved it.

food for the meals we were assigned.

———◆———

Mom and Dad both grew up fishing, so it was natural for them to take their kids fishing, too. Some of the family's favorite places to go fishing are in Colorado, Florida, and Canada. Mom loves fly-fishing, but she doesn't like it where we usually fish in Aspen, because it's "catch-and-release." Despite her being, as she describes herself, "little Miss Person who feeds every critter on the face of

Grilled Vegetable Marinade

■ BY MATT DUDNEY

¾ cup olive oil
⅓ cup balsamic vinegar
1 teaspoon garlic powder
1 teaspoon salt
½ teaspoon white pepper
½ teaspoon dried oregano
½ teaspoon dried basil

Mix thoroughly. Marinate vegetables for one hour before grilling.

SERVINGS: 4 TO 8

This works great with sliced zucchini and yellow squash.

God's earth," she does like to eat the fish that she catches. "I don't like to catch it and have to release it. I like to eat fish. Of course," she laughs, "Ken says that I often release the fish even before I've landed them!"

———◆———

When we go to Aspen in the summer, we sometimes do what they call "packing in." You ride on horseback and the guides lead you up the mountain. The ones really "packing in" are the mules, which carry all of the supplies. There's a base campsite at

Blackening Seasoning

■ BY MATT DUDNEY

If you plan to grill or broil meat on your camping trip, blackening is a simple way to season it. You can purchase blackening seasoning at the grocery store, but I prefer to make my own. That way I can control the ingredients and change the flavors to suit what I'm cooking. This recipe works well with all meats. Use it as a starting point, and then experiment with different spices until you create the flavor that suits you best.

¼	cup paprika
3	tablespoons garlic powder
1	tablespoon onion powder
2	tablespoons celery salt
1	teaspoon cayenne
1	teaspoon ground thyme
1	tablespoon ground cumin
1	teaspoon chili powder

Mix well in a small bowl.

SERVINGS: 8

about 10,000 feet and then a site at 12,000 feet that's the usual spot for lunch. The whole journey is breathtakingly beautiful with the mountains and forests and amazing meadows. The guides prepare wonderful meals (so it could hardly be called "roughing it"). Along the way, there's a beautiful spot for fishing and, since it's on private land, you get to keep your fish and eat them, which, of course, makes Mom very happy.

On the last outing, Mom naturally felt the need to do her customary feeding of the horses, and, especially, "those poor little mules." So she went out into a field and picked giant handfuls of this luscious grass and kept bringing it over to the horses and mules. Later, she found out that they had "packed in" Oreos and marshmallows as part of the provisions. So she started sneaking those treats to the animals. "They loved me, especially those mules," Mom laughs. "I just had the best time feeding the horses and mules."

This kind of camping is quite different from what the Dudneys usually do. "I'd never thought camping could be so fancy because when we camp we do all the work," Mom says. "Well, in this case, they did it for

Roast Beef

■ BY MATT DUDNEY

I recommend preparing any meat ahead of time when going camping. It makes cooking easier in the woods. I like to prepare roast beef in advance. If you cook it before you go camping, the meat has a longer storage life. You can use it for sandwiches, cut it up for soups or stews, or slice off a piece and heat it over the fire. Cooking it first saves time and trouble, so make it in the comfort and convenience of your kitchen at home.

3-pound roast
Olive oil
Chopped fresh rosemary
Garlic powder
Salt
Black pepper

Rub roast with olive oil. Sprinkle liberally with rosemary, garlic powder, salt, and pepper. Place in a roasting pan. Bake in a 350° oven until an internal temperature of 140° is reached. Allow meat to rest for ten minutes before slicing. Serve on sandwiches or with gravy and potatoes.

SERVINGS: 6

I normally use top round for this recipe.

Beef Jerky

■ BY MATT DUDNEY

Everybody in our family insisted that I include this next recipe because they like it so much. My family snacks on salty things, rather than sweets, and one of their favorites is beef jerky. If you go to the store to buy it, you'll be shocked at how much some dried-out seasoned meat can cost. Make your own beef jerky for about one-tenth of what the store-bought version costs, and you'll have a product that doesn't contain any preservatives or MSG.

Ken and Nathan enjoying the scenery of Sheep Creek, Washington.

1	3- to 5-pound roast, trimmed and sliced ⅛-inch thick
¼	cup Worcestershire sauce
¼	cup soy sauce
2	tablespoons A-1 Steak Sauce
2	tablespoons mustard
2	tablespoons barbecue sauce
1	teaspoon ground ginger
3	tablespoons Louisiana-style hot sauce
1	teaspoon onion powder
1	teaspoon garlic powder

In a bowl mix all ingredients and marinate meat in refrigerator for 24 to 36 hours. Place drip pans in the bottom of the oven. Place beef strips directly on baking racks and dry for up to 18 hours (bake on lowest setting) in an oven that is held open, near the handle, by a dish cloth or a hot pad. Remember, you are drying the meat. Cook until dry but flexible, not crispy like bacon. There are many variations to the marinade; be creative.

SERVINGS: 4

I usually select a roast for my meat, but no one ever said that you could not make jerky from any dark meat such as venison, duck, or pheasant.

138

us, and that left me much more time to pick grass and gather Oreos and marshmallows for the mules and horses, so that was fun.

"A lot of people only like this kind of camping. I, on the other hand, am happy in just a tent with our food and bed on the ground."

Well, maybe, but Mom blows her case with this admission: "I have a butane curling iron and I sit in my tent and I take my mirror and set it up there and I put my makeup on—full blown makeup—and I take that curling iron, with the butane that heats up and in just three or four minutes it's hot, and I just sit there and curl my hair. We're miles from modern conveniences and anybody who might care how you look, but, tah-dah, when I come out of that dressing room, I mean tent, I'm ready to dazzle the great outdoors."

Ken taught Matthew how to water ski while camping in Washington state, 1976.

◆

I like to go fishing in Canada, but it's usually not with my parents. I go with Aunt Louise's husband John and a group of friends, including our family dentist. The Canada trip is everyone's favorite, largely because of the "shore lunches." When you fish with a guide, he will land the boats at lunchtime and cook for you.

For my first "shore lunch" we landed the boats, built a fire, and cleaned some fish. The guide brought out the largest frying pan that I had ever seen and placed it on the fire. Next he opened canned potatoes, which he sliced along with some fresh onions. Then he took the cleaned fish fillets and dropped them into a bag of breading. Everything was

all right so far, but I wasn't too thrilled about the canned potatoes.

Here's where things got ugly. The guide unwrapped these one-pound blocks of fat that looked like butter, but were the wrong color. He placed them in the frying pan atop the coals of the fire. I was curious about what he put in the pan, so I asked my friend George what it was. It was lard. I lost my appetite. I had never eaten anything cooked in lard and I wasn't ready to start. On the other hand, I didn't want to offend our guide by abstaining. So in the end I took a taste.

Fried Pancake Fish

■ BY BARBARA MANDRELL

Trout has always been one of our favorite catches. The first trout I remember eating came from a small stream in Washington state, while we were camping and attending the Dudney family reunion. We would catch the trout in the early morning and eat them for brunch. Our Aunt Martha Stifter gave Mom this recipe for fried fish. It's outstanding!

Pancake mix
24 ounces fish fillets
1 lemon

In a bowl mix pancake batter for four servings, according to the directions on the package. Dip the fish fillets in batter. Fry in a deep-fryer or in a skillet until golden brown and serve with lemon wedges.

SERVINGS: 4

You can use any type of fish normally served deep-fried. I prefer this recipe with trout or walleye.

To my surprise, this dish was by far the best fried fish I had ever eaten. The fried potatoes and onions had a delicious flavor and texture. After we had finished eating, I was ready for the next day of fishing just so I could eat another one of these "shore lunches."

When I returned home to Nashville, I told my parents about these amazing shore lunches. It turns out they had a similar experience when they went fishing, and while they too were leery, they thoroughly enjoyed their shore lunch cooked in lard. I went to the grocery store later and bought some lard of my own.

Nathan's first encounter with cooking . . . mud pies, 1986.

Breading Mix

■ BY MATT DUDNEY

This breading mixture will make your fish come alive with flavor. The best way to apply the breading when camping is to place it in a plastic bag, add the fish, and shake well. This way you don't make a mess and you haven't wasted any breading mix.

3	cups breadcrumbs
1	teaspoon garlic powder
1	teaspoon salt
½	teaspoon white pepper
½	teaspoon dried oregano
2	tablespoons chopped parsley

In a bowl mix ingredients well.

SERVINGS: 8

You can also use this mix to bread meats and vegetables. It's really great for pork chops.

Irlene with her first deer and a wild boar, Texas, 1998.

Wild Game

*O*ur family loves the outdoors. At home we feed turkeys, other wild birds, squirrels, deer, raccoons, and opossums. We even have a special feeding stand outside a window so we can watch raccoons and opossums eat.

While everyone in my family fishes, only a few of us hunt. My mom, for example, is not against hunting, but it's not something she will ever do. Aunt Louise and Aunt Irlene and their husbands, John and Rob, all hunt, as do Nathan and I.

All family members, regardless of whether they hunt, support a policy that no one kills any game animal unless they plan to eat it. We have never liked the idea of killing an animal just for sport. The joys of a hunt are in the companionship and beautiful scenery that you encounter when out in the wild.

Even if you do not hunt, you can purchase duck, quail, and other wild meat at many grocery stores. I hope that you enjoy these recipes as much as we do.

> **W**e have never liked the idea of killing an animal just for sport. The joys of a hunt are in the companionship and beautiful scenery that you encounter when out in the wild.

Louise, Barbara, and Irlene shooting sporting clays on their "three sisters vacation," 1999.

*A*unt Louise and John live on a scenic farm in Ashland City, Tennessee. It covers almost five hundred acres. Water, most notably the Cumberland River, surrounds almost all of their property. There are a couple of dozen ponds on the property. The rest of the land is laid out upon tall hills and lush valleys.

It's a wonderful place just to spend time. Aunt Louise and John raise cattle and keep horses there, but it's such a large piece of property that there's plenty of space to enjoy hunting. Through the years, family members have created some delicious dishes from the harvests of our hunting.

I particularly enjoy spending time on the property and planting food for the quail, deer, and wild turkeys that live there. Aunt Louise and John are involved with the Tennessee Wildlife Resource Association. With the TWRA's assistance, they have created the proper habitat for the animals that live on their land. It's a very harmonious place.

———◆———

My favorite type of hunting is duck hunting. Nathan always wanted me to take

Champagne Quail

■ BY MATT DUDNEY

John and Aunt Louise often throw parties for their friends and family and frequently ask me to cater for them. One of Aunt Louise's favorite game dishes is quail. I created this recipe just for her and it's become a staple around her home.

6   quail, well-rinsed
2   tablespoons honey
1   teaspoon Dijon mustard
1   tablespoon barbecue sauce
1/2 teaspoon garlic powder
     Salt and pepper to taste
1   small can mandarin oranges, drained
1   small can crushed pineapple, drained
1/4 cup sparkling wine

Make a boat out of aluminum foil and place the quail in the boat. In a bowl mix honey, mustard, barbecue sauce, garlic powder, salt, and pepper together. Place oranges and pineapple around quail and top with honey mixture. Add wine. Bring edges of foil together and fold to seal. Bake in a 375° oven for 35 minutes and serve with wild rice.

SERVINGS: 6

Aunt Louise loves this recipe. I make it for many of her dinner parties.

him hunting when he was young, but Mom would never allow it. The year Nathan turned twelve, he was invited by Eli Bennett, a dear friend of the family and one of Dad's business partners, to go to Eli's hunting preserve in Arkansas. Dad and I could not believe that Mom allowed Nathan to go. Arkansas has some of the best duck hunting in the world, and Nathan, knowing how special the place was, could hardly contain his excitement about the trip. Nathan was also happy because he was allowed to bring his dog, Dandy, a yellow Labrador. And Dandy was excited because she got to see her mother, Honey, who is Eli's dog.

The first day out we had no luck at all and Nathan was becoming a little frustrated. He

Louise with her "corina" fish, Saltonsea, California, 1965.

Stuffed Saffron Quail

■ BY MATT DUDNEY

You can substitute any of these quail recipes with a small game hen. Hen works just as well, but make sure to increase your cooking time because these birds are usually larger than quail.

2½	**cups white wine**
¼	**teaspoon saffron**
1	**teaspoon dried rosemary**
2	**cups chopped olives**
2	**cups cooked white rice**
1	**small onion, minced**
½	**teaspoon salt**
½	**teaspoon pepper**
6	**whole quail, euro-boned**
1	**cup olive oil**
2	**cups sour cream**

In a saucepan bring white wine, saffron, rosemary, and olives to a boil. Lower flame and simmer for five minutes. Strain olives, saving liquid. In a bowl mix olives, rice, onion, salt, and pepper together. Stuff quail with mixture and close the cavities with toothpicks. Rub birds with olive oil and place in a roasting pan. Add olive liquid to remaining olive oil and pour into roasting pan. Place quail in a preheated 450° oven. Reduce the heat to 300° and roast for 30 minutes, basting often. Remove from oven and strain fat from basting juice. Mix sour cream and basting juice in a saucepan over low heat. Simmer until thick. Serve by splitting quail and topping with sauce.

SERVINGS: 6

Grilled Duck with Cranberry Wine Sauce

■ BY MATT DUDNEY

4	duck breasts with skin
¾	cup red wine
¼	cup cranberry sauce
1	stick cinnamon
3	whole cloves
1	tablespoon chilled butter

Duck: Grill, skin side first, until cooked medium rare to medium. Allow meat to rest for five minutes before slicing on a bias.

Sauce: In a saucepan reduce wine, cranberry sauce, cinnamon, and cloves by one-third. Strain mixture and return liquid to heat. Bring to a boil and finish by stirring in butter.

SERVINGS: 4

This recipe goes great with Matt's fig stuffing.

was in the process of learning a skilled hunter's most important attribute—patience. Eli had told Nathan, "You can shoot whatever you want, but you will eat whatever you shoot." While being patient, Nathan heard a bird overhead. He eagerly prepared the shot, and with a keen eye and a steady hand, shot and dropped the bird! It was the first thing he had ever bagged on a hunting trip. Nathan later admitted that *woodpecker* really didn't taste so bad.

The next day Nathan got lucky (that is, he showed his natural hunting skills) and took a beautiful speckled belly goose. Since it was Nathan's first "real" kill, the goose was taken to a taxidermist and mounted. (Our cat Kumaté did not like the new addition to her home.)

Irlene with her "corina" fish, Saltonsea, California, 1965.

Fig Stuffing

■ BY MATT DUDNEY

½ loaf white bread, cubed
1 cup cream
¼ cup blended whiskey
¼ cup sliced figs
1 teaspoon salt
½ teaspoon white pepper
1 pinch grated nutmeg
¼ cup clarified butter

In a bowl mix all ingredients and bake in a large casserole dish in a 350° oven for 35 minutes.

SERVINGS: 4

———◆———

Likewise, my first trip was also memorable. My grandfather Irby took me pheasant hunting in California when I was eleven years old. It was special enough just to be going hunting with my grandfather. But this trip was especially fun because our hunting companion was none other than the King of Cowboys himself, Roy Rogers. Talk about a dream come true for a kid of any age—it's a

Matt's Easy Orange Duck

1   clove garlic
3   oranges, peeled and sectioned
1   duck
$^1\!/_2$ teaspoon salt
$^1\!/_2$ teaspoon white pepper
$1^1\!/_4$ cups orange juice
$^1\!/_3$ cup Grand Marnier
$4^1\!/_2$ teaspoons grated orange zest
1   tablespoon butter

Place the garlic and orange pieces inside the duck and rub with salt and pepper. Bake in a 350° oven for two hours on a roasting pan with a drip rack. Baste often. Remove from oven and strain fat from juice. In a saucepan cook duck juice, orange juice, Grand Marnier, and orange zest over high heat until thick. Add salt and pepper and finish by stirring in butter. Serve with orange slices and sauce.

SERVINGS: 2 TO 4

Matthew teaching Louise how to break down a duck.

Kumaté and her new-found housemate (the mounted goose from Nathan's first hunting trip).

precious memory of mine now. We also used Roy's hunting dogs. Anyway, sure enough I bagged my first pheasant that day. (As with Nathan's goose, my first pheasant was not eaten, but stuffed and mounted high in the rafters at Fontanel.)

And what kind of shot was Roy Rogers? Well, my grandfather and I wanted to do a little trap shooting after we finished hunting. We talked Roy, who at first was reluctant, into going with us. Roy stepped up with his shotgun and commanded, "Pull!" The target flew, Roy aimed effortlessly, pulled the trig-ger, and broke the target. He strode over, sat the shotgun down, and said, "O.K." We reckoned he'd made his point well enough. It simply wouldn't have been the "cowboy way" for him to keep shooting.

◆

Again, you do not have to be a hunter to enjoy the flavors of wild game. Check your local grocery store for duck, goose, or quail. If you're looking for venison, call your local meat market or butcher. If they don't have it in stock, they should be able to order it for you.

Roast Goose

■ BY MATT DUDNEY

Nathan has yet to take another goose, but when he does, we are going to use this recipe. I've assured Nathan that he can cook it all by himself.

1	pound Italian sausage
½	cup sliced mushrooms
½	cup chopped celery
1	small onion, chopped
1	small goose

Remove the sausage from its skin and mix with the vegetables in a bowl. Stuff inside of the goose and close with toothpicks or sew with baker's string. Bake uncovered for ten minutes in a 450° oven. Reduce heat to 350° and bake covered for 1½ hours, basting often. Carve and serve with stuffing.

SERVINGS: 4

Try this with my Italian Stuffing on page 38.

Matt's Dirty Rice

3	cups chicken stock
½	onion, sliced
½	cup chopped celery
1	clove garlic, minced
½	pound chicken livers and giblets
1	tablespoon butter
1½	teaspoons oil
½	onion, chopped
1	celery stalk, chopped
½	large bell pepper, chopped
1	cup long grain brown rice
	Salt and pepper
	Cayenne pepper
¼	cup fresh parsley, chopped

In a saucepan bring stock to a boil with one-half onion, one-half cup of celery, and garlic. Add livers and giblets, lower heat, and simmer until livers are just done, but still pink inside. Drain, reserving stock. Coarsely chop livers and edible giblets and reserve. In a large skillet melt butter with oil. Sauté one-half onion, one stalk of celery, and bell pepper for five minutes. Add rice and sauté two minutes more, stirring constantly. Add 2¼ cups reserved stock, bring to a boil, cover, lower heat, and simmer until rice is almost done (20 to 30 minutes). Season with salt, pepper, and cayenne to taste. Add reserved livers and giblets and continue cooking until rice is done. Garnish with chopped parsley.

SERVINGS: 6

Marinated Venison Medallions

■ BY MATT DUDNEY

Another family first in hunting happened recently. Aunt Irlene went deer hunting for the first time in 1998 and brought down a beautiful buck. She had never prepared venison before, so she asked her husband's mother for a recipe. Some folks prefer to make chili or steaks out of venison but this recipe is delicious.

1	*venison tenderloin, cut into medallions*
¼	*cup teriyaki sauce*
1	*teaspoon ginger powder*
	Salt and pepper

Irlene shoots as good as she looks.

Prepare the marinade of teriyaki sauce, ginger, and salt and pepper (to taste). Marinate the venison medallions for at least one hour prior to cooking. When ready, grill the medallions until they reach an internal temperature of at least 130° (this will cook them to rare). Allow the medallions to rest for five minutes before serving.

SERVINGS: ABOUT 4

See my recipe for teriyaki sauce on Page 160 and serve these with my Garlic Mashed Potatoes on Page 120.

Matthew and his parents at "Magnolias," a restaurant which they own with friends in Franklin, Tennessee.

A Chef in the Family
Gourmet Cooking Made Easy

The word *gourmet* might make you nervous. It makes most people nervous. Well, I decided to look it up in the dictionary, and it turns out that a gourmet is nothing more than "a connoisseur of fine food and drink." How could that be scary?

Now, if I really apply this definition, my grandmother is a gourmet cook. She's what you might call a Southern gourmet. My mom is also a gourmet cook. Her sisters are gourmet cooks. The point is, being a gourmet is something any of us can do. All we have to do is love food—both eating and preparing it. And that's something all of us can do.

In this section you will learn some of the tools and the tricks that professional chefs use in their kitchens to make food preparation easier. The tools I discuss are not exotic; they're just simple things such as knives and spoons, and pots and pans. The important thing is not to have a *lot* of tools, but to know how to select and use the *right* tools.

Most of the techniques I discuss apply to preparing and cooking sauces. That's because sauces are the basis of so many great cuisines. You can easily learn to make all of these sauces with the tools you already have in your kitchen. And all of the ingredients you'll need are commonly available in most grocery stores.

> "**B**eing a gourmet is something any of us can do. All we have to do is love food—both eating and preparing it."

Although I've worked in several styles of restaurants and I've learned different cooking styles from a variety of world-class chefs, I've found that they all use a few, classic sauce preparation techniques. You'll find that when you employ them, the time you save will allow you to enjoy yourself and be creative.

Finally, as you prepare your meals, remember what we've said before—you are cooking for someone that you care about, so relax and enjoy yourself. And remember, good food is gourmet food.

*T*he recipes in this section are easy, yet the resulting dishes are the kind you might find in a fancy restaurant. These recipes will teach you techniques that you can use repeatedly when you are preparing foods. The good news is that the more times you use a particular technique, the better you will become at it, and consequently, the more proficient at cooking you'll become. (Remember: Practice makes perfect.)

Tools for the Kitchen

During my years as a professional, I've learned to create with a minimum of tools. A few in particular are the only real essentials for the kitchen. If you use them, you'll save time in the kitchen, and cooking will seem easier and more enjoyable.

Let's start with knives. If you test the ones in your kitchen, you'll probably find

Danny Egnezzo's Marinara Sauce

■ BY MATT DUDNEY

This particular recipe came from a professional chef and dear friend of mine, Danny Egnezzo, but I had to promise that I wouldn't share the exact ingredients with anyone, so I changed it slightly. My mom loves this red sauce and says it's the best she's ever tasted. I'll let you be the judge.

1	large onion, chopped
2	tablespoons olive oil
1	tablespoon crushed garlic
1	16 oz. can plum tomatoes, peeled
1	tablespoon fresh oregano, chopped
2	tablespoons fresh basil, chopped
1	dash sugar
	Salt and white pepper

Using a soup pot, sauté onions in olive oil, adding garlic when onions begin to turn transparent. In a bowl crush the tomatoes. Add the tomatoes to the onions and continue to cook over medium heat. Add oregano, basil, and sugar once the sauce begins to bubble. Cook for about 30 minutes. Salt and pepper to taste.

SERVINGS: 6

Because I use this for so many dishes, I usually make it in bulk and freeze it for later use.

that most of them are dull. The best way to put an edge on a knife is by using a whet stone and mineral oil, or a special knife sharpening oil. If you don't know how to use a stone, have your knives sharpened by a professional. Never use the knife sharpener on the back of an electric can opener. It can irreversibly damage your knives.

Your kitchen might have a wooden block that holds many kinds of knives, but only two are essential to your kitchen: a chef's knife and a paring knife. A chef's knife (usually about 10 inches long) covers more surface area and finishes the job faster than a shorter knife. It's my favorite for general-purpose cutting. A paring knife has a short blade with a curved or tapered point. I like to use it for peeling.

Chef's assistant Nathan helps Matthew prepare a family dinner.

Roux

■ BY MATT DUDNEY

| 1 | *pound butter* |
| 2 | *cups all-purpose flour** |

In a saucepan melt butter and bring just to the point of smoking. Using a whisk, mix in the flour while stirring briskly. The mixture will begin to thicken. Continue to add flour until the mixture becomes very thick but smooth, not lumpy.* Remove from heat and allow to cool. Or add stock to make a gravy or sauce.

MAKES ABOUT 20 OUNCES.

The amount of flour will determine the thickness of the roux.

A roux is used to thicken sauces, soups, and gravies.

Chicken Parmesan

■ BY MATT DUDNEY

1   *egg, beaten with ¼ cup water*
4   *boneless chicken breasts*
     Breading mix
4   *slices Provolone cheese*
4   *teaspoons Parmesan cheese*
4   *servings cooked spaghetti*
2   *cups marinara sauce*

Bread chicken using breading mix and an egg wash. Deep-fry or fry in a skillet. Finish cooking in a 350° oven. Place cheeses over chicken while hot and serve over pasta. Pour on sauce and complement with a hot loaf of bread.

SERVINGS: 4

Eggplant Parmesan

■ BY MATT DUDNEY

3   *pounds sliced eggplant,*
      breaded
     Oil
3   *cups marinara sauce*
1   *pound Provolone cheese, sliced*
¼   *cup grated Parmesan cheese*

Buy the eggplant already sliced and breaded (or prepare it yourself with a breading mix and egg wash) and fry lightly in a saucepan with oil. In a large casserole dish layer ingredients as follows: eggplant, sauce, Provolone cheese, Parmesan cheese. Repeat. You should get three layers, finishing with the cheeses. Bake in a 350° oven until well heated and all the cheese has melted. Allow to cool for ten minutes and serve.

SERVINGS: 8

I serve this to people who say they don't like eggplant. I don't tell them what it is and they love it.

If you feel you need more than two knives in your kitchen, a boning knife and a bread knife are good choices. A boning knife has a thin, pointed end used for boning meats and poultry. A bread knife is long and thin with a serrated edge. But again, you'll need only a chef's knife and a paring knife to prepare most meats and vegetables.

Quality in your equipment is critical. My dad taught me long ago that when buying any kind of tool, you should purchase the finest you can afford in order to decrease the likelihood you'll have to buy it again. This goes for kitchen equipment as well. (Quality tools you buy today can be in the kitchens of your children

Nathan, Danny Egnezzo, and Matthew in Barbara's kitchen preparing dinner for Barbara and Ken. Nathan has found his brother's love of cooking.

Old-Style Meatballs

■ BY MATT DUDNEY

1	*pound ground beef*
½	*cup breadcrumbs*
1	*small onion, minced*
1	*red bell pepper, minced*
1	*teaspoon garlic powder*
1	*teaspoon salt*
½	*teaspoon white pepper*
1	*tablespoon Worcestershire sauce*
1	*egg, beaten*

In a bowl mix all ingredients together. (Add another egg if not moist enough.) Form into 2-inch balls. The meatballs should have the same consistency as hamburgers. Bake on a wax paper–lined jelly roll tray for 35 minutes in a 350° oven.

SERVINGS: 4

and grandchildren!) Even a quality kitchen knife can last a lifetime if you take proper care of it. Knives made of German steel seem to hold up best with daily use. If you choose to buy professional-type knives, wash them by hand. A dishwasher can damage them.

Now, let's turn to the pots and pans. I love to cook on stainless steel pots, or copper pots lined with stainless steel, because

Thai Tuna Mix

■ BY MATT DUDNEY

1   *can tuna in water, drained*
1   *stalk celery, chopped*
½   *can water chestnuts, thinly sliced*
      Salt and pepper
      Garlic powder

In a bowl mix all ingredients together and chill. Serve as is, or with a Thai coconut sauce (as shown above).

SERVINGS: 2

they are great at conducting heat and respond well. But they are expensive. If you can afford it, buy them. But it's not essential. You can use your everyday pots and pans. However, stay away from aluminum cookware because food will stick, and aluminum pots often ruin the flavor of food.

Non-stick pans are great to have on hand, but they don't work for all types of cooking. Non-stick coating is easy to destroy, so be gentle when cleaning the surface.

Now, there are just a few other tools you should consider having around. Strainers are handy for draining pasta, vegetables, oil, sauces, and a hundred other uses. You'll need a large strainer for pastas and a small strainer for sauces. Most professional chefs use a strainer called a Chinois (sheen-wah). This is a cone-shaped, fine-mesh strainer used exclusively for stocks and sauces. They tend to be expensive—anywhere from $70 to $150. And although it's money well spent, it's a lot to spend on one strainer. If it's going to blow your cookware budget, you

Thai Coconut Sauce

■ BY MATT DUDNEY

½   can coconut milk
2   dried chili peppers
1   orange
½   lemon

In a saucepan heat the coconut milk and chili peppers. Roll the orange and lemon on a countertop to aid in juicing. Halve the fruit and squeeze the juice of one-half of the lemon and the entire orange into the coconut milk. Place the leftover orange and lemon pieces in the coconut milk. Bring to a boil and reduce by half. Chill before serving.

SERVINGS: 2

Thai Cabbage

■ BY MATT DUDNEY

1   tablespoon sugar
2   tablespoons rice wine vinegar
1   teaspoon sesame oil
     Salt and white pepper
1   head savoy cabbage, chopped

In a large bowl mix the sugar into the vinegar. Add the oil, salt, and pepper. Toss the cabbage in the mixture and chill before serving.

SERVINGS: 2

Japanese Shrimp Teriyaki

■ BY MATT DUDNEY

1   cup diced eggplant
½   cup sliced shiitake mushrooms
1   cup sliced button mushrooms
1   pound shrimp, shells removed
1   teaspoon soy sauce
1   teaspoon rice wine vinegar
3   tablespoons teriyaki sauce
    Salt and white pepper

In a skillet lightly sauté vegetables in oil, adding shrimp when vegetables are halfway cooked. When shrimp start to turn pink, add the soy sauce and stir. Next, deglaze the pan with the vinegar and finish by adding the teriyaki sauce. Season with salt and pepper to taste and serve over bean threads, rice, or noodles.

SERVINGS: 4

Teriyaki Sauce

■ BY MATT DUDNEY

½   cup soy sauce
2   tablespoons sugar
1   dash ground ginger

In a saucepan bring soy sauce to a boil while adding sugar and ginger. Reduce heat and simmer for five to ten minutes until desired consistency is reached.

SERVINGS: 4

can use cheesecloth over your regular strainer instead.

Finally, high-temperature rubber spatulas, whisks, and tongs can make life easier in the kitchen. You can find them in kitchen supply stores or cooking equipment catalogs.

Secrets of Making Sauces

Sauces are the basis of many dishes, and therefore it's worthwhile to learn how to prepare them well. Most professional chefs use sauce techniques and secrets that you can adopt at home to save you time and make food preparation easier.

Most cooks use cornstarch or flour to thicken gravies. But the resulting gravy can sometimes come out lumpy. When using cornstarch, you should always mix it with a small amount of cool water, and use your hand to eliminate any lumps. A gourmet secret most people don't know, however, is that arrowroot will also thicken gravies and soups in the same way but is less likely to form lumps.

When I use flour to thicken sauces such as milk or breakfast gravy, I make a slurry first. A slurry is simply a mixture of liquid and flour. The type of liquid used depends

Chicken Fried Rice

■ BY MATT DUDNEY

It's easy to expand upon the simplicity of preparing fried rice. I use chicken here, but you might want to use pork, shrimp, lobster, or beef.

1	cup chicken, cut into thin strips
	Oil
½	cup cooked peas
½	cup chopped carrots, blanched
½	onion, diced
¼	cup chicken stock
6	cups cooked white rice
2	tablespoons soy sauce
1	egg, beaten
	Salt and pepper

In a large skillet sauté chicken in oil, adding vegetables when chicken is three-fourths of the way cooked. When chicken is done add chicken stock and rice, mixing well. Chicken stock will reduce. At that point add soy sauce and toss well. Add egg, salt, and pepper while mixing. Serve when egg is completely cooked. For a meatless version, heat only the rice and oil in a large sauté pan over medium high heat. Add the vegetables and soy sauce. Stir well. Add egg, salt, and pepper, and continue mixing. Cook until egg is done. Serve hot.

SERVINGS: 4

on the type of sauce you are making. For milk gravy you would make a milk slurry. For soups and sauces, you would probably use a water slurry.

Another thickener used by professional chefs is called a roux (pronounced "roo"). A roux is a mixture of butter or oil and flour. When stirred briskly over high heat, it creates a mixture used to thicken soups and stews. Chefs use roux primarily in French and Cajun cooking. But I've included a simple roux recipe in this chapter that you can use in lots of creative ways.

If you've made a sauce and it starts to "break" or separate (that means the oils are separating from the rest of the sauce), don't throw it out. You can easily bring the sauce back by adding a small amount of very cold

Lobster Club Sandwich

■ BY MATT DUDNEY

This recipe shows you how easy it is to take an everyday sandwich and turn it into a gourmet experience.

1   4-pound lobster
1   teaspoon lemon juice
    Salt and white pepper
2   tablespoons mayonnaise
6   slices toasted bread
6   slices tomato
1   avocado, sliced
8   slices cooked bacon

In a pot, boil lobster until bright red and chill in an ice bath. Remove tail and claw meat from the lobster. Tear the lobster meat into large chunks and toss in lemon juice. Salt and pepper to taste.

To build the sandwich, spread mayonnaise on outside pieces of bread and layer between them as follows: lobster, avocado, bread, tomato, and bacon. Cut in half and serve.

SERVINGS: 2

water and vigorously whisking it in.

At most fancy restaurants, chefs serve their most elegant dishes with classic sauces. If you want to recreate these sauces at home, you can find prepackaged powders that mix with just water. And those are fine when you're in a rush, but I've given you some fast and easy recipes in this chapter for making the real thing. I guarantee it will taste better. The more often you make a sauce, the better it will get. So practice, practice, practice!

Marinara sauce is what chefs call a "mother" sauce. That means it's a sauce from which you can make other sauces. Marinara sauce is the basis of many Italian dishes, and making it in quantity will allow you to save time. Just divide it up, freeze it, and then use it as a base for spaghetti, meat sauces, peppers and sausage, lasagna, stuffed shells, raviolis, pizza, and whatever else you can come up with. The secret is simple: When you're making a meal, make extra sauce. I freeze the remainder in plastic freezer storage bags. If you fill them to the point where they lie flat with no bulge and then freeze them lying down, the bags will stack easily in your freezer. This is a great way to save space and you can thaw only what you will be using for the next meal. I've included several recipes in this chapter that will make use of all your frozen marinara sauce.

One simple recipe is spaghetti with meat sauce: first brown the ground meat and drain the oil, then add one of the frozen bags of marinara sauce. It doesn't even need to be completely thawed before you put it in the saucepan. Heat and serve over pasta.

Asian food is also a sauce-based cuisine. And it's very easy to cook, once you've prepared the ingredients. You can't always replicate the exact dish you've had in a restaurant, but you can create a variety of

Anchovy Butter

■ BY MATT DUDNEY

½   teaspoon anchovy paste
¼   cup softened butter
½   teaspoon lemon juice

In a small bowl fold the anchovy paste into the butter while adding the lemon juice. Chill until firm and cut into chips. (The method is found in the "Dill Herbed Butter" recipe, page 164.)

SERVINGS: 4

Japanese Salmon

■ BY MATT DUDNEY

6   ounces salmon fillet
1   carrot, thinly sliced*
1   yellow squash, thinly sliced*
1   zucchini, thinly sliced*
    Salt and pepper to taste
1   teaspoon soy sauce
1   tablespoon butter

Make an aluminum foil boat. Place salmon and vegetables in boat. Top with seasonings and butter. Seal foil and grill or bake in a 350° oven for about 12 minutes. Place foil on plate to serve.

SERVINGS: 1

*The vegetables will have to be very thinly sliced in order to cook in the short amount of time required.

Dill Herbed Butter

■ BY MATT DUDNEY

1   teaspoon chopped dill weed
¼   cup butter, softened

In a bowl fold the dill weed into the softened butter until well mixed. There are two methods for chilling:

Using plastic wrap, mold the butter into a round loaf and wrap it. Place the butter in the freezer. When firm, remove from plastic wrap and slice into chips.

Or, using wax paper, spread the softened butter to a one-third-inch thickness and place on a cookie sheet. Chill in the freezer until firm. Form the butter chips using a small cookie cutter. The chips will peel easily from the wax paper.

Notes: Here is an opportunity to be creative. Use whatever combination of herbs and spices you create. Here are a few ideas: ground cumin, horseradish, Tabasco sauce, seasoning salt, garlic powder, crumbled bacon, chopped chili peppers . . . whatever you can create.

SERVINGS: 4

Grilled tuna with herbed butter, served with home fries.

great sauces simply from bottled spices and sauces you buy at the grocery store. I've included a number of great recipes in this chapter to get you started and help you practice with Asian food.

Another simple sauce trick that will come in handy when you serve grilled or broiled fish is herbed butter. It's easy to prepare, and all you have to do is top your ordinary fish with it and you've created a gourmet fish dish. You're enhancing the flavor of your food with nothing more than a little butter mixed with some spices. And the best part is the flavor possibilities are endless.

Finally, these are just a few easy recipes and the basic tools and techniques you need to create them. Pick a handful of recipes that appeal to you

Matthew and Barbara at "Magnolias."

Fresh Mussels in White Wine Sauce

■ BY MATT DUDNEY

Here's an elegant dish that's easy to make and guaranteed to impress your dinner guests.

1	dozen fresh mussels, rinsed and drained
¼	cup white wine
3	tablespoons minced tomatoes
1	tablespoon minced garlic
1	tablespoon chopped parsley
1	tablespoon butter

In a covered sauté pan steam mussels over high heat in white wine until they start to open. Add tomatoes, garlic, and parsley and toss. Continue to cook until mussels are completely open. Finish sauce by stirring in butter.

Serve in a large bowl with a side of soft bread.

SERVINGS: 1

Roasted Lamb Chops

■ BY MATT DUDNEY

Here is an easy restaurant-style meal to try at home (roasted lamb chops served with garlic cream sauce and roasted red skin potatoes). You can do it.

8   *large lamb chops*
     Olive oil
1   *tablespoon finely chopped fresh*
        rosemary
1   *pinch garlic powder*
1   *pinch salt*
1   *pinch pepper*

In a bowl toss the lamb in the oil. Place lamb on a roasting pan and lightly coat with spice mixture. Bake in a 350° oven, turning twice during cook time. Most people eat lamb rare to medium rare. The internal temperature will be 140° for rare and will take about 15 minutes. Allow meat to rest for three minutes before serving.

SERVINGS: 2

This recipe is great for grilled chops, too.

Garlic Cream Sauce

■ BY MATT DUDNEY

1   *pint heavy cream*
1   *clove roasted garlic*
     Salt and white pepper

In a saucepan bring the cream and garlic to a boil. Reduce heat and simmer until desired consistency is reached. Season, strain, and serve warm.

SERVINGS: 4

This is a sauce you can use in a squeeze bottle to decorate a plate.

and try them. Become comfortable with them and then pick a few more. After that, try a little experimenting. Remember, cooking is supposed to be enjoyable. It's easy, it's gourmet, and I'll bet that when you make these dishes, nobody will be asking you to wash the dishes afterwards. Enjoy and have fun!

Classic Roasted Red Skin Potatoes

■ BY MATT DUDNEY

12	medium red potatoes, cut into wedges
2	tablespoons clarified butter
1	pinch salt
1	pinch white pepper
1	tablespoon fresh rosemary, finely chopped
1	pinch garlic powder

Matthew with friend Danny Egnezzo at Danny's restaurant in New Jersey.

In a bowl toss the potatoes in the clarified butter while adding the spices. Make sure that the spices are evenly distributed. Bake the potatoes in a 375° oven on a jelly roll tray for 10 to 30 minutes, depending on the thickness of the potatoes.

SERVINGS: 4

$\mathcal{I}$ndex